· POPULAR ·
· COLLECTABLES ·

toys

· POPULAR ·
· COLLECTABLES ·

toys

Kevin McGimpsey
&
Stewart Orr

GUINNESS PUBLISHING

Acknowledgements:
*The authors would like to thank
Maureen Quayle, Ray Simpson and
Robert Mann.*

Editor: Honor Head
Picture Research: Julie O'Leary
Design and Layout: Steve Leaning
Photography: Chris Brickwood

Published in Great Britain by
Guinness Publishing Ltd,
33 London Road, Enfield, Middlesex

Typeset in Caslon Old Face
by Ace Filmsetting Ltd, Frome,
Somerset
Printed and bound in Italy by
New Interlitho SpA, Milan

**British Library Cataloguing in
Publication Data**
McGimpsey, Kevin
  Toys. – (Popular collectables).
  1. Toys. Collectors' guides
  I. Title II. Orr, Stewart III. Series
  745.592

ISBN 0-85112-923-4

contents

INTRODUCTION
pages 6–8

TOYS

a	pages 10–22	*j*	page 73	*s*	pages 106–115
b	pages 23–30	*m*	pages 74–92	*t*	pages 116–126
c	pages 31–51	*n*	pages 93–97		
d	pages 52–71	*p*	pages 98–103		
g	page 72	*r*	pages 104–105		

MANUFACTURERS

a	pages 128–129	*g*	page 147	*m*	pages 158–166
b	pages 130–136	*h*	page 148	*p*	pages 167–170
c	pages 137–143	*i*	page 149	*r*	page 171
d	page 144	*j*	page 149	*s*	pages 172–176
e	page 145	*k*	pages 150–151	*t*	pages 177–179
f	page 146	*l*	pages 152–157	*v*	page 180

SPECIALIST SERVICES

Toy Fairs   page 182

Magazines   page 183

Toy Shops   pages 183–184

Clubs & Associations   page 185

Display Cabinet Makers   page 186

Toy & Doll Museums   page 187

INDEX
pages 188–192

introduction

Why collect toys?

One of the main motivations for collecting toys is nostalgia. Most people remember their childhood days as being happy and hold memories of the playroom or the box of ever-changing toys. However, the nostalgia factor can often result in random toy collecting, accumulating everything and anything that the adult had as a child, whether that be a Hornby tank train, a Dinky Supertoy or a Pedigree doll. Such toys are often bought as a commemoration of a happy youth. On the other hand, one sometimes reads in the newspapers about specialist toy experts who began collecting as a child – usually these are theme/brand name collectors.

Lastly, the investment factor cannot be ignored. Although the majority of today's toy collectors vociferously deny that they are in the hobby for the investment, it should be remembered that toy values seldom go down and that some day a toy collection may be sold, not by the present owner but more likely by a beneficiary. Everyone likes a bargain and conversely nobody likes to pay more than they must for a toy. Several investment-orientated specialist antique toy shops have been established throughout the world offering toys as alternative investments to stocks and shares. In such shops prices for toys, in mint condition and where relevant with boxes, are high and seldom reveal any bargains. The investment factor is not necessarily a completely negative one, but the influence of investors has forced up prices to such an extent that new and established collectors are hard pressed to pay the asking prices.

Which toys to collect

So what is there to collect and how does the budding enthusiast become a toy collector? It is a good idea to build upon what you have already – a box of model cars, a couple of dolls etc., and of course you should truly enjoy your subject matter. Remember that old can be combined with new. A collector of old Dinky model cars, for example, can enlarge his collection with the Dinky model cars being produced by Matchbox Toys today.

This book covers many of the different types of toys that are available, but bear in mind that older toys are going to be harder to find and will invariably cost more than present-day toys.

Where to buy toys

The most obvious source for old toys is shops that specialise in such items, many of which advertise in hobby and model magazines (see page 183). Some may concentrate on just trains or dolls whilst others will have a wider selection of collectable toys, but most will be only too happy to advise and give direction to new collectors. As part of their service to collectors such shops are often happy to take toys in exchange for others, and to keep faith with the clientele they will often buy back toys at a very reasonable price.

A large selection of fairs for obsolete toys are now organised at weekends throughout the country. Once again, they are advertised in model magazines and of course the local press. Many of the larger fairs such as the Farnham Maltings Toy Show in Farnham, Surrey, or the Windsor Toy Fair held in Slough, Berkshire, offer the collector the opportunity to buy collectable toys from well in excess of 100 stallholders (for further details see page 183). Stallholders may be specialist retailers who have taken surplus stock to the fair for the day or collectors who are thinning out their collections. Invariably asking prices are somewhat less than shop prices and because it is a market the stallholders are happy to haggle over the asking price. A word of advice – see what is on offer from all the stalls, compare the prices, identify what is of interest to you and then negotiate.

Other sources are the classified advertisements in magazines such as *Exchange and Mart* or the local press. Jumble sales and boot fairs provide the opportunity to chase a bargain!

What price to pay

It has to be remembered that, like most antiques, collectable toys are subject to the laws of supply and demand. In recent years collectors have been rigorously chasing the toys available and as this supply has diminished so prices have risen. It is up to the individual to decide how desirable the toy on offer is and if the asking price can be justified. Remember that everything always sells, that if you don't buy the toy then someone else will and that today's ridiculous price may look like a bargain within a few years. Notwithstanding this, there are two main factors that have an obvious bearing on the asking price of a toy: condition and rarity. As to the former, the better the condition the more desirable and so the more costly.

Toys are, after all, only children's playthings – inevitably they become broken or scratched. Toys that have survived in pristine condition are an exception and will always be the collectors' preference. In recent years, partly due to the investment factor, many collectors will only consider buying a toy that is mint and boxed (where relevant). The ultimate is a toy that is as it left the factory: no paint blemishes and clean complete original packaging. Such a toy is undoubtedly much easier to sell back to the specialist traders, but the same toy without its box is not. It may be hard to comprehend but in some cases the box can be worth as much as 50 per cent of the toy! Not everyone can afford to collect mint and boxed toys and indeed may not want to anyway. What about a toy in not such good condition? Two schools of thought exist: On the one hand, it is best to keep the toy in the condition as bought until one comes along in better condition, as often the toy in inferior

introduction

condition can be used as a part exchange for the toy in better condition. On the other hand, some collectors achieve much satisfaction from restoring the toy to its former glory, but as a general rule collectors would prefer a scratched original to a good repaint!

If this strikes the reader as an odd fact of life, consider that the very high value of most obsolete diecast toys is often because they had unusual colour finishes which established their rarity. Most diecast toys are extremely robust and seldom actually fall apart, so a restoration, no matter how good, must ruin the original reason for its high value. The individual not concerned with investment can gain much pleasure from restoring and displaying a toy for which very little would have been paid.

Rarity is a relative thing. All old toys that have survived to the present day are rare, as the vast majority were eventually discarded by bored children and then thrown away by their parents. Rarity in specific terms is more relevant when looking at categories of similar toys, e.g. Hornby trains, Dinky model cars, dolls etc. Trains such as the Hornby Princess Elizabeth made in 1938 were very high in quality but low in quantity – however, although this train is relatively rare, many of them have survived intact because it was a costly toy that from the start commanded respect and care.

Photographs and valuations

All the photographs produced for the book have an accompanying description and estimated price. This price, which is of course based on the authors' opinion, is the amount that you would expect to pay at a collectors' shop or other specialised outlet.

It will be noted that where a toy has been described in a caption as being boxed or not the value reflects this, and so the price given relates to the actual item photographed and not one like it or a pristine example of the same thing. All estimated prices are correct at the time of going to press and the publishers cannot accept any liability for loss, financial or otherwise, incurred by reliance placed on the information given. Where there is more than one item in a photograph, the caption reads from top to bottom or left to right.

Generally, the toy collector puts a large premium on any toy which was originally boxed and this can be double the value of an item where the box is missing. This particularly applies to diecast toys but holds true for most other types of toy as well.

Throughout the book a Dinky road sign measuring 2 inches in height has been included in all the photographs. This should give the reader an idea as to the differing sizes of the featured toys.

toys

· AEROPLANES ·

The aeroplane was invented at the turn of the century, with the first successful flight being recorded in the USA in 1903. It did not take long before the manufacturers were making replicas. All were made in Germany by toy companies such as Bing (q.v.), Marklin and Gunthermann (q.v.).

TINPLATE

The pre-World War I toys were all made from tin and the majority had clockwork engines linked to the propeller. Although these aeroplane toys were not intended to fly, some of the toy manufacturers linked them to a pole or column and by means of a clockwork engine the toy aeroplane could fly in a continuous circle. These early toys varied in size from just under two feet in wingspan down to inches for penny toy aeroplanes. Pre-war aeroplane toys are often fragile and nearly impossible to find. They are highly collectable and command extremely high prices.

Between the wars and after World War II civilian airliners became the fad of toy manufacturers. Every year records were being set and broken by the airlines – the longest non-stop flight; the number of passengers; the most remote country etc. Most of the major countries were promoting their own airline companies and it was regarded as good free advertising to see toy aeroplanes in the toy shops with their livery rather than those of their competitors.

During the 1930s many models were issued based on real aeroplanes that were being developed in the lead-up to World War II. The two leading toy manufacturing countries, Japan and Germany, made a vast range of single-seater fighter planes, long-distance

bombers and seaplanes. Many were
painted in camouflage and often looked
just as sinister as the real subject.

Extras such as battery, lights, landing
equipment or spark-effect firing guns
and engine noises were incorporated
into late-1930s toy aeroplanes. After
World War II the Japanese continued to
make sophisticated battery-operated, as
opposed to clockwork, aeroplanes,
although after the peace treaty was
signed they concentrated solely on
civilian airliners. By the 1960s Japan
had successfully introduced plastic
components into their toy aeroplanes
such as propellers, cockpits and
wingtips. These were added not only as
a cost-saving exercise but also to comply
with contemporary consumer safety
regulations.

Most aeroplane collectors have a fair
knowledge of the history of this form of
transport and it is this that usually
initiates their interest. Many will prefer
to collect examples of a certain scale but
this is very restrictive and no common
scale is evident. The collector should
ideally be able to carry out simple
repairs as toy aeroplanes are fragile, as
much a reflection of their shape as
anything else. Aircraft are difficult to
display as they are quite bulky. Many

The constructor sets from
Meccano were only
produced before World
War II and were not
overly popular. The
number of special parts
they contain make them
rare and collectable.
Illustrated is the impressive
Number 2 Bi-plane, £200
boxed

collectors hang them from ceilings but this is far from ideal; on the other hand, large examples can take up a lot of room if displayed in cabinets. Realism was difficult to achieve and perhaps not a dominant consideration when these toys were made in the past, but today the main factors are the size, sophistication and working features of any example.

Manufacturers
Compagnie Industrielle du Jouet (q.v.), Fleishmann (q.v.), Gunthermann (q.v.), Marx (q.v.), Mettoy (q.v.), Schuco, TN (q.v.).

DIECAST
The most prolific producer of diecast aeroplanes was without doubt Meccano Ltd of Liverpool. The first, released in 1934 under the Dinky (q.v.) trademark, was an Imperial Airways liner. Most of the early civilian liveried aeroplanes were militarised in 1938 when the outbreak of war seemed imminent. Dinky aircraft made before the war were found to be suffering from metal fatigue – some of the impurities in the alloys caused the metal to crack and eventually disintegrate. This fatigue had been rectified by the late 1940s when

A Bi-plane from an unidentified English maker, this is a well-preserved example from the 1930s; £225

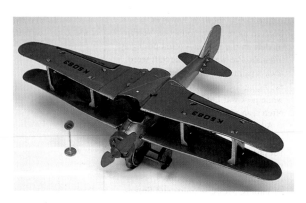

TOP TO BOTTOM
An Avro York from Dinky
c 1949, is a relatively
common item, but in fine
condition is worth £70
boxed.
This boxed example of the
famous Flying Fortress by
Dinky dates from 1938.
Being free from the
dreaded metal fatigue, it is
worth £150 boxed.
The Vickers Vanguard is
also a sought after model;
£75 boxed

the production of both Dinky vehicles
and aircraft continued. Many aircraft
made in the pre-war years were reissued
in the immediate post-war period
although they were always reissued in
different colour schemes. The most
famous Dinky aircraft was the Avro
Vulcan Delta Wing Bomber made in
1955. Only 500 were made and the
majority were given to the aircraft
manufacturers. A genuine mint and
boxed example of this model would
fetch over £1000 at an auction. In 1985
a Vulcan model that had been resprayed
was sold at Phillips Auction House and
realised £400! Beware, however,
because there are reproduction Vulcan
models on the market – often posing as
originals. Pre-war Dinky aircraft were
always painted – blue, green, yellow and
red being the most common colours,
while post-war Dinky aircraft were more
often than not issued in a silver finish.

A large-scale Dinky aircraft range was
introduced in the 1970s and although
not popular with collectors at the time
they have in recent years become
collectable. Models of Spitfires,
Phantoms, Messerschmitts and Stukas

were produced up to the end of Meccano in 1979. As detailed representations of the actual aircraft they are without doubt very accurate but being rather large they do not have the quaint charm of Dinky aircraft made between the 1930s and 1960s. Mettoy Playcraft made a small range of Corgi (q.v.) aircraft in the early 1970s. These are not very collectable at this time.

Lesney Products (q.v.) have also made a range of diecast model aircraft under the brand name of Sky-Busters. They were introduced in 1973 and are still being produced in 1989. With the demise of Dinky, the Sky-Buster range was the only range of diecast models aeroplanes being made by a British toy manufacturer. Matchbox Toys continue to recolour the older models and introduce on average two to three new models every year.

Pre-war Dinky aircrft are subject to metal fatigue. Dinky models with original boxes command high prices but unboxed models will always be in demand.

Manufacturers
Dinky, Matchbox (q.v.), Mettoy (q.v.).

· AEROPLANE ·
· CONSTRUCTION ·
· KITS ·

In 1931, just before Meccano (q.v.) introduced their Dinky range of diecast aircraft models, they launched a complementary range of construction kits of aeroplanes, boats and cars based on the principle of Meccano. The aeroplane sets consisted of a quantity of blue and white pressed tin sheets, fittings, nuts and bolts. Different aeroplanes could be made from one kit as the parts were interchangeable between the sets numbered No. 00 to No. 2 Special. Aeroplane constructor kits made close to the outbreak of World War II were often painted in camouflage and are regarded as being more collectable than the earlier civilian aeroplanes. These kits were not reintroduced after the war.

Undoubtedly, the introduction of plastic kits by Airfix (q.v.) reduced the sales of diecast aircraft. A more detailed and authentic-looking aeroplane could be assembled by the enthusiast and often the price of a plastic kit was less than a diecast aeroplane model.

A further example of construction kits is the famous Frog range of aircraft, produced by International Model Aircraft Ltd and marketed by Lines Bros. Models were made from wood, paper and wire and each plane, once assembled, could be flown after using the winder in the side of the box which wound up the rubber band attached to the propeller. Although only a relatively few people collect Frog aeroplanes, high prices are often obtained for mint condition examples. Obviously the majority of aeroplanes made did not survive as invariably the ones that were flown between the 1930s and 1960s crashed!

Aeroplane kits are only just becoming collectable with a mere handful of dealers specialising in them. While an area such as this is in its infancy prices stay low, but equally large stocks of kits will be soaked up by these traders. The time to buy is now. The other problem to be aware of is that the moulds for manufacturing plastic kits cost huge sums initially but the cost of remaking them is low and so there is always the danger of a reissue: *See also: Constructor Kits.*

Manufacturers
Dinky (q.v.), Frog, Meccano.

· AIRFIX ·
See Manufacturers

· ANIMAL ·
· FIGURES ·
METAL

The firm of W. Britains Ltd (q.v.) launched a large range of farm animals in 1923. Known as the Model Home Farm series, it was created as a result of

Accessories such as this pond add realism to the background figures and are quite rare and desirable; £70 the set

falling sales in their lead soldiers due to the growing anti-war feeling in the country in the aftermath of the battlefield horrors of World War I. Britains also realised that the farm animal figures would have just as much appeal to girls as they would to boys. The animals were made to the same scale as the lead soldier figures, i.e. approximately two inches high, and were popular with train collectors and enthusiasts as they added realism to their train layouts. The figures were extremely well made and were passed from generation to generation. By the outbreak of World War II Britains Ltd had over 60 different animals in their Model Home Farm series. During the war, when few if any toys of any type were being made, it was common for such animal figures to be repainted and given to the refugee children to play with. The range had been extended by 1939 to include farm workers, farm vehicles, haystacks, trees, drinking troughs and even sacks of corn. Wooden buildings were also added by Britains.

After seeing the immediate success of these animal figures, Britains launched their Hunting Series – two different sets featuring huntsmen and women, horses and hounds. These sets are difficult to find today. Zoo animals then followed as well as animals and figures associated with a circus.

Inexpensive and fragile yet extremely nostalgic. Animal cut-outs such as these from the 1920s are worth £15 each

Britains animal figures are plentiful and inexpensive. These are examples from the 1930s and 1940s; £6 each

Lead figures made by Britains are marked as such underneath the base of the figure. Several other British manufacturers made lead animal figures – the most significant company being John Hill Co. Although not as collectable as Britains figures they are still sought after by collectors.

W. Britains Ltd also produced a range of farm figures and animals in their Lilliput series. They were made to OO gauge and were aimed at model railway enthusiasts. Although road-going vehicles had been made during the immediate pre-World War II period, the figures and animals first appeared in the early 1950s. Some early boxes containing the Lilliput range were marked as being made by W. Horton – this was a subsidiary of W. Britains Ltd who initially made the figures and animals. By 1954 the range was made by Britains with no mention of Hortons. The series was extensive and included a land girl, stable lad, farmer and wife, shire horses and a collie dog. There are many colour variations to be found on the animals and figures as many manufacturers used out-workers to paint the models (Lesney Products is just one) and these all add extra interest for the collector.

Lead figures from this era have a charm all their own, not least perhaps because they were made from a material which is now totally banned in the manufacture of toys.

One of the most famous figures from the Britains era is that of the village idiot. It came into existence, or so legend has it, because Queen Mary upon seeing the range at a trade toy show in the early '30s is thought to have said: 'The only thing missing is the village idiot.' Britains promptly produced the figure but it was not popular and was withdrawn after a couple of years.

Unless the figure has been kept as a collector's piece from the start, most will be found with some paint loss. Of course a mint example is more desirable but figures in a lesser state will always be of interest to the collector. As with most toys it is best to resist any ideas of repainting or restoring the figures unless they are so bereft of paint that they are sore on the eye!

PLASTIC

Many plastic animal figures have been made since the 1950s when the plastic injection moulding technique was mastered by many of the leading toy manufacturers. Britains saw this as an opportunity to revamp their farm series and at the same time make them less expensive to manufacture by changing from metal to plastic. The 'Herald' series of farm animals was launched in the early 1950s and in recent years this brand has become highly collectable. Many are over 35 years old and evoke nostalgic memories for a whole generation of children who would never have played with lead figures.

During the early 1950s Britains acquired shares in Herald Miniatures and this led to a merger of the two firms in 1956. Between 1956 and 1959 Herald Miniatures produced their own range of plastic figures including the set known as the 'Antarctic Explorers'. This very rare set was made to commemorate the 50th anniversary of the reaching of the South Pole. In fact, there were two different sets – the Polar Sledge Team and the Polar Survey Party. Both sets came with husky dogs, which were also sold loose. In 1959 Britains and Herald combined their products in one catalogue. By 1953 Herald had introduced an extensive range of plastic farm animals – these included rabbits, cats, goats, calves and lambs and are all eagerly sought after by collectors.

Britains continue to this day to make a large range of farm and zoo figures – all sold singly or in sets and affording much pleasure to today's generation of children. Britains farm animals in plastic are always marked as being Britains and should not be confused with the cheaper imports from the Far East such as Hong Kong.

Britains catalogues, which are now collectable in their own right, are valuable sources of product information.

WOOD/PAPER

The firm of Raphael Tuck still make a range of paper/cardboard animals fitted to rocking mechanisms. These date back to the turn of the century and were popular with Victorian and Edwardian children. Tuck made a vast range of paper cut-outs designed for children to compile educational scrapbooks.

TINPLATE

Most examples of animal figures made

from tin were fitted with clockwork mechanisms and in most cases are categorised as novelty toys.

OTHERS

The substance known as Elastolin had been perfected by such firms as Hausser, who made a vast range of zoo and farm animals during the 1930s. These are very collectable.

Manufacturers
W. Britains Ltd (q.v.), Hausser (q.v.), Herald Miniatures, Timpo (q.v.).

· AUTOMATONS ·
See Battery Toys

· ARKS ·

Wooden Noah's Arks have always been a popular toy. They were most common during the reign of Queen Victoria and were bought as both an educational and a religious toy. Generally toys were not to be played with on Sundays by Victorian children, but the exception was Noah's Ark which was permitted due to its religious connection. The size of the ark can vary from under 12 inches in length and up to 15 pairs of animals and the two human figures, to the larger size of over 24 inches and with up to 100 pairs of animals. The shape of the ark was usually a house resting on a boat. Often they were painted to give a representation of a two-storey ark. The roof or the walls of the house could slide off to hold the wooden animals and birds. The vast majority of wooden arks were made in Bavaria, Germany, but they were also made in Sweden and the USA. Noah's Arks are very collectable and can often be found for sale in various degrees of

Wooden Noah's Arks are amongst the oldest collectable toys, predating even the era of tin. This one, thought to have been made in 1839, is a perfect example of both a religious and instructive plaything; £450

condition. Arks decorated with inlaid wood or straw-work are eagerly sought after by collectors. The animals and birds are often lost or damaged. Although the paint on the older arks does tend to fade, in no circumstances should the paintwork be renovated. Damaged animals with broken limbs can be successfully repaired by the collector.

Very often a Noah's Ark can be bought cheaply because there appear to be few that were manufactured by actual companies and even fewer with a known company trade mark. A Noah's Ark could easily be built by a carpenter, joiner or home handyman and so many beautiful examples are rather anonymous, appealing only on their merits rather than on their heritage. Unrecognised by the antiques trade, they tread an uncertain line between a general antique and a toy.

· BANKS ·

Often referred to as money-boxes, banks are more often than not classified as collectable toys. There are two main categories: still banks and mechanical banks.

STILL BANKS

As the term implies, the still bank quite simply stores coins and, unlike the second category, does not have any play value. Still banks are usually made from porcelain, china or tin. Common themes include typical English cottages, pigs and red post office boxes. The former would have appealed to both adults and children, whereas the latter would have been made purely for children.

MECHANICAL BANKS

The vast majority of these ingenious money-boxes were made in the USA between the late 1890s and the early 1920s. The most common material used was cast iron. Although produced to enable children to save their money, these banks afforded much fun and pleasure because when the coin to be saved was put in or on a certain part of the bank it activated a movement or

Illustrated here are two American Money Banks made of cast iron which means they are virtually indestructible. The seated figure is known as a Tammany Bank; c £150. The Jolly Nigger, although socially unacceptable in an enlightened age, is worth about the same

movements. For example, the Bear Bank made in the 1870s invited the child to roll a dime (or penny) down the rifle barrel held by President Theodore Roosevelt. A bear concealed in a tree trunk then appeared!

Many of the subject matters were based on topical events such as political scandals. One of the most famous mechanical banks is known as the Tammany Bank – this showed William Boss Tweed sitting in a chair, and the coin used to activate him quickly disappears into his pocket. He had been arrested in the early 1870s for defrauding a political party in New York. Being a famous scandal of its time, many thousands of this bank were made.

During the 1960s and 1970s reproduction and fake mechanical banks began to appear on the market. Often these were crude copies, made in the Far East, with tell-tale signs of their origin being mainly bright colours of new paint. The fakes then became more sophisticated and the colours were faded down. They are now often very hard to spot and to a certain extent have made it more and more important to buy only from a reputable expert. Most of the original designs were patented by the designers and were backed up with drawings and diagrams. This 'background' information has, over the years, been made available to bank collectors and dealers and enables them to accurately check dimensions, colours etc. to help detect forgeries.

Knowledge has to be gained before any serious purchase is made. Beware of general dealers who claim that what they are selling is not a reproduction as this implies that they know all about reproductions, which is really not possible.

· BATTERY ·
· TOYS ·

German tinplate toy manufacturers used batteries in their more sophisticated toys during the 1920s and 1930s. This increased their play value but was limited to powering car headlights or flashing emergency vehicle lights or sirens. The true battery-operated toy really came to the fore during the 1950s and 1960s. Japan became the biggest producer of such toys and these are often described by toy experts as modern-day automatons. The battery replaced the tedium of having to rewind wound-down toys and toys could entertain children for longer periods of time. The Japanese proved to be expert at making toys that moved by the use of ingenious yet cheap mechanisms and small electric motors. Cheap, as always, implies unreliability and much of the value of a battery toy today lies in whether or not it still works or can be easily repaired. Many Japanese toys of that era were made from recycled tin and cloth, yet their appeal is in the cleverness of their construction. By the 1970s the Japanese were quick to respond to the challenge of safety regulations and also the demands of increasingly more sophisticated children by turning their attention to computer games and more inter-active toys; however, battery toys are still being made in the early 1990s. The Chinese toy producers frequently copied early Japanese toys, and some experts have forecast that Chinese modern-day battery toys will in time become as valuable as Japanese toys. However, collectors do not have such a high regard for them due to their greater use of plastic and often inferior design.

There are two distinct groups of

This amusing model of the Frankenstein monster is a rare example of the classic battery toy from Japan. The simple electric motor drives a cam which causes his trousers to fall down and his face to light up in embarrassment—clever but fragile because of cheap materials used; £150

This classic 'Highway Patrol' tinplate car was produced in many forms. Generally, the larger the rarer and the fewer plastic parts the better. This late 1950s example is in working order; £100 boxed and appreciating rapidly

Charlie Weaver was produced in huge quantities mainly for the American market but the toys were not made to last. These increasingly collectable figures came in several forms and are appreciating rapidly from £60 unboxed. The Circus Lion is unusual but still appeals at £100 unboxed

battery toy: figures – animals, people and robots; and vehicles – cars, aeroplanes, boats and trains. Battery toys in the latter group were made predominantly from tin, whereas the former group could consist of not only tin but also celluloid, plastic, rubber and cloth (for the costumes).

When considering the purchase of a battery toy, always insist that the vendor shows you the toy working. If necessary carry a couple of batteries with you in case a lack of batteries is given as an excuse not to see the toy operating. There are two main factors that determine the value of a battery toy: condition – try and buy a battery toy that is in the best possible condition, one that does what it is supposed to do and preferably with its original box. Use the information on the box as a checklist of what should come with the toy. And desirability – the most sought-after toys are robots, cars and figures.

Manufacturers
Alps (q.v.), Bandai (q.v.), Gama
(German) (q.v.), Ichiko (q.v.), Linemar
(q.v.), T.N. (q.v.).

· BOATS ·

Collectable toy boats as opposed to
model boats were generally made from
tin rather than wood. Model boats tend
to be scaled-down accurate replicas
whereas toy boats have more charm due
to their often disproportionate sizes and
colours. Early toy boats were not
intended to be 'sailed'; instead they
were often fitted with removable wheels
to enable the child to 'sail' his boat on
the carpet.

Tinplate boats dating back to the turn
of the century are extremely valuable –
even a boat in a rusty and distressed
state will be of value. They also retain a
value even if they have been totally or
partially restored. However, they are
expensive and are seldom seen for sale
other than in specialist shops or at
specialist auctions. The more desirable
boats are those dating before 1910, of
German origin, big in size (up to 36
inches) and fitted with a steam-driven
mechanism or sophisticated clockwork
engine. However, tin boats dating from
just before World War II can sometimes
be found and these too are worth
having. Small tinplate clockwork boats
from the early 1950s made in Germany
by companies such as Arnold often fetch
prices well in excess of £300. The world
record price obtained for a tinplate toy
was an 1885 Marklin boat called the
'Imperator' which sold for £125,000 in
1989.

Sutcliffe Pressings based in Horsforth
near Leeds began making wooden and
tin boats in the 1920s. Although these

Sutcliffe maritime toys are
the most common of all
toy boats but are
becoming increasingly
collectable; £25 each

These two Hornby clockwork boats are from 1938. Although rare, they do not command the high prices normally associated with Hornby products because they have less visual appeal. The Venture was the best of the range; £120. The Racer is worth £60

This Battleship by Lehmann dates back to 1920. In this poor condition it is worth only £75

do not compare in quality with the boats made by German manufacturers such as Bing, Marklin or Fleishmann, they are still collectable and can often be found for quite reasonable prices. Sutcliffe boats were first made in the 1920s and were fitted with a small methylated spirit lamp which, when fired, boiled up water in the copper tubing which was expelled under force at the stern causing the boat to move forward. Cool water from the pond or lake was in turn taken on board automatically. By the end of the 1920s Sutcliffe introduced clockwork boats to their range of battleships and speedboats. The Sutcliffe range was never vast and

reissues and remakes of original boats continued until the demise of the company in the late 1970s. Many of these boats made in the 1950s and 1960s are the most common of all tin boats – simple clockwork mechanisms, small in size (less than 12 inches) and often fitted out with plastic figures one of which includes Sooty, the television puppet. They are not expensive because they are very basic and rather unimaginative in their design but they may be a collectable range in the future.

Hornby also made a range of clockwork tin boats before World War II. These are eagerly sought after not only by boat collectors but also collectors interested in Meccano products from Liverpool. Their first boat was made in 1932. Although not comparable in design with the German toy boats, the 'Venture' Limousine-type boat, which measured 16.5 inches in length, was normally painted in red and cream and featured an enclosed cabin, windows, seats and steering wheel made from celluloid. A powerful clockwork engine made the Venture a dream boat to sail with a range of nearly 300 feet! Hornby also made a series of speedboats and a cabin cruiser (Viking).

Tri-ang made a range of large-scale plastic clockwork boats during the 1950s and 1960s. The subject matters were usually of civilian lines, and although made out of plastic these have become

This Tri-ang radio controlled cargo ship belongs to the first generation of plastic mouldings in toy making; it was therefore constructed with a far higher degree of care than is normal today. This range of model boats will be the collectors' pieces of tomorrow although their electronics are already completely outdated by today's standards; c £60 in this condition, boxed

The American 'Baby Wee' has a rugged simplicity and charm all of its own; £95. A pre-war German Liner such as this has great appeal, mainly because of its excellent lithography; £85

well respected by boat collectors in recent years. They are often seen with missing parts or unboxed and these factors have a detrimental effect on the value.

Ironically, tin is very susceptible to rust and a boat that has been in the water is nearly bound to suffer from this. Plastic is of course completely impervious, so nearly any tin boat is valuable simply because it has survived! Naval examples are more interesting than civilian and of course the older the better.

Manufacturers
Arnold (q.v.), Bing (q.v.), Fleishmann (q.v.), Hornby (q.v.), Sutcliffe (q.v.), Tri-ang.

This accurate RAF Tender was produced by the somewhat eccentric Victory Industries concern in the 1950s. Of limited appeal now but it will be sought after in the future. Worth £65 boxed

· CARS ·
TINPLATE

Collectable cars made from either tin or diecast date back to the turn of the century. Toy manufacturers saw an opportunity to capture the imagination of children by making scaled-down versions of cars on the road. Some of the automobile manufacturers also made tinplate toy cars based on their own ranges, an example being the French car manufacturer Citroën.

Tinplate cars made during the golden age of tinplate, 1900 to 1910, are so rare and so collectable that examples in excellent condition can fetch prices in excess of £10,000. Although expensive, the tinplate clockwork cars made during the 1930s and 1940s by such companies as Tipp, Gunthermann and Paya have become some of the most collectable within the toy world. Along with condition, other factors that influence the desirability of tinplate cars are size (the bigger the better), the soundness of the clockwork and/or battery-related mechanism, and how accurate an example of the real marque the toy is. To a certain extent the toy manufacturer is also important and collectors would generally rather have a German tinplate car than a Spanish one, the latter country having a toy manufacturer called Pawa which, although good, was never regarded as being a leading force in the toy world. British toy manufacturers such as Wells or Mettoy (q.v.) are regarded as being less collectable than German manufacturers. Some of the tinplate cars from the 1930s were sold in boxes and this can often give a clue to the toy's country of origin and even what type of car it is. The addition of the box is also of great value in monetary terms.

An excellent model of an MGA by Victory Industries, dating from the mid-1950s. Although made of plastic, it is of good quality. Its value is rapidly appreciating; currently £100

A large and imposing Paya Limousine from the 1930s, powered by a clockwork motor, has recently been remanufactured by Paya. This original example will always be worth more than its re-issues; £600

Tinplate cars based on famous television or film characters are collectable. The German firm of Mangold made a superb James Bond Aston Martin in the early 1960s. During this era, the Japanese toy manufacturers took the lead in tinplate toy cars. Toys based on Cadillacs, Buicks and Chevrolets, all made in great detail and driven by battery motors, now have a very big following, especially in the USA.

Tinplate cars continued to be made after the war. Even though there were raw material restrictions, German toy companies such as Schuco and Arnold continued to make smaller-sized, clockwork and battery-operated tinplate cars of famous marques such as Mercedes Benz and Porsche. Toys from this era in mint and boxed condition are very collectable.

This tinplate Clockwork Saloon by Chad Valley is greatly enhanced by the occupants in lithography. A post-war example like this commands a value of £85

In contrast, this pair of Mercedes Benz 190s illustrates just how realistic a model could be made to look. One example is powered by clockwork whilst the other is battery powered. Mint boxed examples such as these are avidly collected and are worth £220 each

In more recent times, the Chinese have taken over from the Japanese and their ranges, although of little value today, are regarded as being collectable in the not-so-distant future. Many of their toys are direct copies of famous 1950s and 1960s tinplate cars.

It may well pay the beginner to specialise in model cars from a certain country or manufacturer. Mercedes Benz or Jaguars are always sought after although the main market of the Japanese was the USA, so Cadillacs and Buicks dominate.

Manufacturers
Arnold (q.v.), Bandai (q.v.), Gunthermann (q.v.), Mangold (q.v.), Paya (q.v.), Schuco, Tipp & Co (q.v.).

This clockwork car is by Schuco and reflects the popularity of American cars in Europe in the 1950s; £200 in this condition

DIECAST

One of the most popular collecting themes within the world of toys is collecting diecast cars. The earliest examples date back to the early 1930s with Tootsietoys (q.v.) in America and Dinky (q.v.) toys in England being the most famous. They were introduced for many reasons, the main one being that they were cheaper to make due to their size and scale. The diecast content

A similar type of car as the clockwork by Schuco but by Arnold, dating from the early 1950s. Such models as this were often not based on real vehicles but could contain such elements as realistic passengers; £200

A representative group of diecast cars from the major manufacturers. The Spot-On model of the Queen's Phantom V is unique and was expensive at 25 shillings, even when new in 1964. Because of its price not many were bought, so today, even in only fair condition, it is worth £80. The XK120 is by Dinky c 1958; £80 boxed. A Model T Ford from Lesney is not rare and despite its excellence is worth only £20 boxed. The Corgi model of Bluebird, dated 1962, is worth only £20 boxed.

varied from manufacturer to manufacturer but were considerably cheaper than tin and the final finish was in a lead-based paint as opposed to the expensive lithographed finish on tinplate toys.

In Britain, the earliest Dinky cars were not seen as being potentially collectable when launched in 1934; they were intended solely to be trackside accessories for Sir Frank Hornby's trains and rolling stock. However, the popularity of the Dinky cars became so great that they were soon to be marketed as toys in their own right.

The desirability of a diecast car is affected in the main by age and condition. Pre-war and post-war Dinkys up to 1964 in absolutely pristine condition are worth in many cases £100-plus, and no matter the condition they still have a value especially to the collector who cannot or will not pay the top market price. This category of collector will be happy to buy a distressed car instead and restore the model to a near perfect state. Unlike some other categories of toys, touching up the paint and restoration will

dramatically lower the value of the car. Boxes play an unjustified factor in value: collectors will generally expect the car to be mint and with its original box or packaging. This is not always relevant, though, because Dinky cars made pre- and post-war (up to 1951) were not boxed.

In relation to British diecast toy companies Dinky is the most popular range, followed closely by Matchbox, Spot-On and then Corgi. *See also: Constructor Kits; Corgi; Dinky; Lesney; Spot-On.*

Manufacturers
Corgi (q.v.), Dinky (q.v.), Lesney (Matchbox) (q.v.), Tri-ang (Spot On).

· CHARACTER · · TOYS ·

Also known as television/film-related toys, these are made by a toy manufacturer in the light of a popular television programme or movie.

TINPLATE

Tinplate character toys are sought after by both character toy and tinplate collectors. Interesting examples include clockwork toys of Popye the Sailorman made by a variety of American manufacturers during the late 1930s and 1940s, and the Lone Ranger from the popular television series of the late 1950s. When wound up the horse prances round in a circle and the lasso whirls around the Lone Ranger's head. Although tin was considered by many toy manufacturers as being too expensive and was replaced by plastic during the 1970s, tinplate character toys did appear during that period. Large-sized toys of James Bond's Aston Martin, or the Monkeemobile holding

The Lone Ranger—an early example of a toy modelled on a television series and rarely found in the UK—was made by Louis Marx in the 1950s; £90 and extremely collectable

This toy from 1966 would play a pop song by the group the Monkees when wound up. Basically, it was made from tinplate. An unusual toy full of charm and interest; £200

Muffin the Mule was instrumental in founding the fortunes of Lesney. This heavy diecast puppet was to scratch countless pieces of furniture. It was almost impossible to operate, requiring great dexterity. Very sought after as a character toy as well as a Lesney product; £120 boxed

the pop group the Monkees, are very much sought after today. The Chinese toy makers during the 1970s and 1980s made a tinplate and plastic Batmobile car in various colours other than black. These toys are quite common but could be of value in years to come. The biggest disadvantage with tinplate character toys is that they are usually large and thus difficult to display or store, and are expensive.

DIECAST

Diecast character toys are more abundant and are much more reasonable in price. Most of the British diecast toy manufacturers have at one time or another turned their attention to this theme, the most prevalent being Corgi (q.v.). As the toy manufacturer has to buy the rights to make the toy, it is a costly exercise and the manufacturer has to make as many toys as is possible within a given contract period and also before the popularity of the film fades. The scarcity of such toys has been increased by children playing with them and in turn damaging or destroying them. For example, Corgi's Chitty Chitty Bang Bang is a collector's item today as examples in 100 per cent condition are relatively hard to find. This highly collectable model car was released as a Corgi toy in late 1968 and withdrawn in 1972. Although it was an expensive toy in 1968 (£1 2s 6d or £1.12) it did include many novel

features such as jewelled headlights, flip-out wings and four figures from the film. Missing wings and figures have a detrimental effect on the value of the model. Corgi were fortunate with their Batman range of toys, including the Batmobile, Batcopter and Bat Boat, because Batman was shown over a lengthy period of time on television both in the USA and the UK during the mid-1960s. Hundreds of thousands of these Batmobiles have been produced by Corgi but today complete examples of models fetch a premium price and invariably either one or both of the figures have been lost! Matchbox Toys (q.v.) have also made character toys based on the films including *Licensed to Kill*. Although they are of value they do not have the same following as Corgi character toys.

One of the earliest and most famous diecast character toy is the Lesney (Matchbox Toys) Muffin the Mule, based on the animal featured on BBC television during the early 1950s. Lesney bought the rights to produce the miniature puppet toy from the Annette Mills Syndicate and were to make 50,000 of these puppets. Although the programme did not have an international cult following, this toy is popular with collectors due to the associated nostalgia of childhood. Muffin the Mules are often seen for sale, but often without the puppet strings, the string tail and the fragile box.

Produced as a spin-off from the Batman TV series and revitalised by the release of a new Batman movie, this excellent toy is now worth £100 if in perfect condition. It should be noted that, unlike Chitty Chitty Bang Bang, this model was updated in the 70s. The above price refers to the first production runs of the model in 1966

LEAD

W. Britains (q.v.) made at least two highly desirable sets of character figures in the 1930s. The more common of the two sets is Snow White and the Seven Dwarfs which was sold as a set or loose. Parents still recall the days when, as children, they went into their local toy

Hank and Silver King. This is a model of a TV character from an obscure television series from the late 1950s. It is collectable for only that reason; £45 boxed

shop and by spending their pocket-money over several weeks eventually obtained the full set. Much rarer, however, is the Buck Rogers set of six figures. One such set sold for just over £1000 at an auction house in New York in 1985 and would be worth considerably more today.

Lesser-known British toy companies also turned their attention to character toys in the 1940s and 1950s and figures include Mickey and Minnie Mouse, Goofy and Hank the Cowboy.

PLASTIC

Plastic has been used successfully as a medium. Mattel (q.v.) (USA) successfully introduced their *Star Wars* films range of toys in the 1970s. During the late 1980s Mattel followed this with characters from *Masters of the Universe* and *He-Man*. With a turnover of £30 million in these toys they have proved popular with children and collectors. Plastic figures and spacecraft have been produced in large numbers and these were bought not only by interested children but also collectors. Many of the toys in this category are really dolls and can vary in size from 4–16 inches. The themes are varied and although some of the toys may have been made for one country, the obvious one being the USA, many have eventually ended up in the UK. Kenner made a superb set of *Star Wars* dolls including Darth Vader, Fairylite made the *Thunderbirds* puppets and Denys Fisher made a Dr Who figure, girl assistant and Daleks. Of course, with every blockbuster film that is released the chances of a toy manufacturer releasing an associated toy shortly afterwards as a licensed product is the norm. Look how quickly Tonka introduced the Real Ghost Buster car – this has been followed by Ghost Buster guns, figures and station.

As with most collectable toys, the associated box is a great source of information. Unboxed toys tend to lose some or all of their 'bits and pieces' and the box usually itemises everything that made up the toy upon leaving the factory. An example pursued by collectors is the Denys Fisher Bionic Woman (1976) which should come complete with her handbag. The handbag is often lost and as a consequence so is her purse that in turn contains several items including maps, money, mirror and comb. These losses would have an effect on the value of such a toy to a keen collector.

Although these are not of great value today they are steadily rising in price and could well be collectables of the very near future. One further plastic character toy worth looking for is the large-sized (16-inch) Freddy Krueger talking toy made by Matchbox (q.v.) based on the film *Nightmare on Elm Street*. This frightening toy was released in the USA in mid-1989 and almost immediately withdrawn due to the pressure generated by religious groups, parents' associations and the press. Some 40,000 Freddy Krueger toys were released to the trade. Collectors are

Media and parental opposition was forceful enough to cause Matchbox to withdraw this questionable doll from the market in late 1989. Only 50,000 had been sold in the USA—possibly this may enhance its value in years to come. On the other hand, stocks may yet be imported unofficially into the UK and sold off very cheaply. No value is given as no market price has yet been established.

Now regarded as a classic piece of miniature engineering, this Corgi model was a huge seller for the company in 1967. A combination of fragile packaging and easily lost passengers and fittings conspired to make perfect examples very rare. This toy has trebled in value over the past three years and it is now worth £150 in mint and boxed condition

more than happy to pay a premium to obtain the toy.

The desirability of a character toy is related to just how good a replica the toy or model is. Furthermore, the success of the toy relates to how popular the film or television series is. *See also: Plastic Toys; Space Toys.*

Manufacturers
Bandai (q.v.), Corgi (q.v.), Dinky (q.v.), Fairylite, Gama, Kenner, Lesney (q.v.), Marx (q.v.), Matchbox (q.v.), Mattell (q.v.), Mego Corp.

· CONSTRUCTOR · KITS ·

In an effort to provide greater realism than the Meccano (q.v.) system could provide, Meccano produced a range of cars and aeroplanes in kit form from 1931 to 1939. These kits contained many unique pieces and although they used simple nuts and bolts in their assembly, produced a beautiful end result which today exude great nostalgia and charm. The aeroplanes came in basically two sets, No. 1 and No. 2, but each kit could make several alternatives and accessories could be purchased to upgrade the basic set. In 1933 'No. 1 Special' and 'No. 2 Special' were launched and these could produce dozens of different models as they contained special details such as pilots' cabins, windows and moving parts. In 1932 two Motor Car constructor kits were produced along the same principles, and with features such as Ackermann steering, working handbrakes and other realistic and instructive details. Despite the later introduction of smaller car kits these cars did not sell at all well and they were withdrawn in 1940.

Other companies, most notably the Gilbert company of America, have tried this idea. Gilbert produced the Konstructa kit in the 1930s and 1940s. These are generally built from sturdy, heavy materials and their emphasis is on engineering rather than realism. These cars are rarely seen in the UK. *See also: Aeroplane Construction Kits; Cars.*

· CORGI ·

Playcraft Toys, a subsidiary company of Mettoy (q.v.), launched their range of Corgi miniature diecast vehicles in 1956. As the television advertising said at the time, Corgis were 'the ones with windows'. The now famous trademark of the Welsh Corgi dog was chosen for two main reasons: the main manufacturing plant was at the Mettoy factory in Swansea, South Wales, and because the Corgi breed of dog has always been popular with the royal family, which was thought by the Mettoy directors to give the brand an immediate upmarket image!

The Corgi range (launched in the same year as Lesney's (q.v.) Models of Yesteryear range) was to be in direct competition to the Dinky toys range made by Meccano Ltd. Although in

Three early examples of vehicles from this prolific manufacturer. Corgi toys have generally been under-valued, especially in comparison to Dinky toys. This situation is rapidly changing as collectors realise just how well made and detailed these late 1950s vehicles are; £50 each and rapidly appreciating

This Car Transporter is of substantial weight and very 1950s in character. It is worth £70 in boxed condition

later years Mettoy changed direction to cater more and more for their following of collectors, in the early years Corgi toys were aimed solely at children. They continually looked at ways in which to make their models more appealing and by the time the company was forced to close in 1981 they had introduced such extras as jewelled headlights, spring suspension and opening bonnet, boot and doors.

1950s TOYS

Although Meccano maintained that their Dinky toys were made to a constant scale of 1/42, Corgi believed that this was not compulsory. They were convinced that their range of cars should be slightly larger and be somewhere between 1/44 and 1/48 in scale. The first Corgi model was the Ford Consul, which was quickly followed by an Austin Cambridge, Morris Cowley, Rover 90 and Riley Pathfinder. Like Dinky models, Corgis were first produced with a pressed metal baseplate or chassis. This is a good clue to determine the age of a Corgi toy. These early models were also released with mechanisms that had been developed by Mettoy for their tinplate and pressed tin toys, and so the letter 'M' was added to the model number, e.g. the Ford Consul was numbered 200 in the range; the mechanised version was numbered 200M. These motorised models were not very popular with children and they had been totally withdrawn from the range by 1959, However, today they are very desirable and collectors will pay a premium to obtain one.

By 1957 the baseplate was made from diecast and the range had been made more interesting with the inclusion of a Bedford 15 cwt van and a Commer 5 ton Refrigerator Truck. The numbering of the models was such that the different types of vehicles could be categorised within three digits, e.g.: Racing Cars – 150/199; Cars – 200s; Sports Cars – 300/349; Commercial Vans – 400/499; Large Commercial Vehicles – 450/499; Trailers – 100/149. The models were finished in bright colours and although of little interest at the time to the young consumers, many shades of the same colour were produced and these colour variations are of great interest to collectors today. By the late '50s Mettoy were releasing a new model each month. Late 1957 saw the introduction of the first Corgi Major

This Bentley is a superb model of the Continental especially in this colour scheme. The models of famous British racing cars have long been popular with motor racing enthusiasts and exude the charm and excitement of 1950s racing; £40 each boxed

– a much larger-sized model that was comparable to the Dinky Supertoy range. The first Major (number in the 1100s) was the Carrimore Car Transporter, released at Christmas with four cars as the first-ever Corgi Gift Set. The Corgi Major range is a most collectable series.

In 1958 the biggest addition to the Corgi line was a group of military models – both army and air force types. Standard range models such as the Thunderbird Guided Missile were very popular, but were overshadowed by the military models introduced into the Major range such as the Bloodhound Guided Missile sets, followed the next year by the Corporal Guided Missile set. Mettoy were fully aware of what was happening in the world – the cold war between NATO and the Warsaw Pact was a fact of life and the superpowers were close to sending a man into space.

In 1959 the Corgi catalogue cover showed an array of rockets and missiles and was captioned 'Rocket Age Models'. Corgi military models today are much sought after – preferably in mint condition. Broken or badly bent/rubbed missile heads will adversely affect the price of such toys. Mettoy had begun by this time to incorporate spring suspension for their models. The range had become more international with many of the subjects chosen reflecting the ever-growing American market. Two-tone Ford Thunderbirds in green and yellow, Chevrolet Impala police cars and gold-plated Studebaker Golden Hawks (issued in 1960) all added more interest to the line. At the same time agricultural models such as the Massey-Ferguson Farm Tractor were added and – to the Major range – a Massey-Ferguson '780' Combine Harvester.

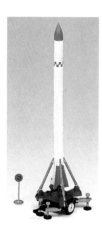

The Rocket Launcher echoes Britain's ambitions for the space age. The model is now worth £70 in boxed condition

1960s TOYS

As with many Corgi models, Mettoy
saw a great opportunity to excite their
young consumer with their replica of the
Bluebird Speed Record Car which had
set a new world land speed record in
1960. This year also saw the first of
several different types of vehicles all
using the Chipperfield's Circus
livery. The first model was that of a
Crane truck which was followed the
next year by a Circus Animal Cage
trailer. This circus series is one of the
most collected Corgi lines – the most
desirable model being the booking
office model which was released in
1962, based on the earlier Mobile Shop.
Chipperfield's Circus Gift Sets were
introduced in 1962.

In 1964 Corgi Classics were
introduced in an attempt to compete
directly with the Lesney Models of
Yesteryear range. The decision to break
away from the normal Corgi practice of
making contemporary miniature
vehicles with a line of classic vintage
models did little to harm Lesney sales.
In total, ten models were released until
the demise of the Corgi Classics in
1969. The quality and detail of many of
the large Classics was of the highest
standard. Several of the models were
reissued in the early 1980s using the
original tooling. The popularity of the
original Corgi Classics has varied and
can be bought today for relatively low
prices. This sub-range could well be a
very collectable line for the future.

Mettoy really put Corgi on the map
when their policy of making popular
television or film vehicles was initiated
in 1965. This type of toy is often
referred to by collectors as a charcter toy
or a TV-related toy. The first of its type
for Corgi was the Saint's Volvo 1800 as
driven by Simon Templar. This was

These beautifully made Corgi Classic cars were originally produced in 1967 and relaunched unsuccessfully in the 1980s. The originals are surprisingly undervalued by today's standards and can be found for £35 each

quickly followed by the Aston Martin driven by James Bond in the film *Goldfinger*. Unlike the Volvo which had no 'extras' the Aston Martin featured James Bond and one of his adversaries holding a gun, both figures being made from plastic; an ejector seat that catapulted the latter figure from the car; an opening roof; a flip-up rear bullet deflector screen and retractable machine guns. Many of these gold-coloured Aston Martins have survived but many are without the plastic figures. Such a loss can severely affect the desirability of this model.

Mettoy could see from the sales of the Bond car that there was an untapped market for character toys. The Dinky range did pose some opposition, but this did not prevent them launching the Avenger Set – featuring the John Steed Bentley (basically the Corgi Classic model) and the Emma Peel Lotus Elan. Each of these models was issued as a gift set. Such a set can only be claimed to be 100 per cent complete if it still has the three small plastic umbrellas which slotted into three holes beside Steed's car! The Man From U.N.C.L.E. Oldsmobile car featuring Napoleon Solo and Ilya Kuryakin was also released in 1966. The more common colour of car is blue, the harder-to-find version is white. All these 'Gun-Firing Thrush-Buster' models were issued with a Waverley ring showing the two agents and this sought-after item often goes missing! The last character toy of 1966 was the Batmobile. This very popular model, made until 1979, had two main features – a three-stage rocket-firing mechanism and a tyre slasher cutting blade at the front. Three yellow plastic rockets could be fired by pressing a button. Robin and Batman sat in the car. Later on Corgi were to add a Batcopter, Batbike, Batboat and Trailer. During the rest of 1967 further character toys were released including *The World of Wooster* Bentley, the *You Only Live Twice* Toyota, the *Dakari* Gift Set (1967), the *Green Hornets* and *Black Beauty*.

In 1968 more character toys were successfully introduced, the most important being the Chitty Chitty Bang Bang car. Also a new version of the James Bond Aston Martin was introduced. Slightly larger than the gold version, this model stayed in the range until the early 1980s. This was then followed by the Monkees' Monkeemobile. The Monkees were an American pop group who for a while rivalled the Beatles in popularity. The Beatles were also introduced into the Corgi range with their yellow submarine in 1969. Many examples of this toy survive but more often than not without the Beatles figures.

1970s & 1980s TOYS

In 1970 the Corgi range was revamped.

This model is perhaps only popular because of the fascination that Beatles memorabilia attracts. The original cartoon provided a somewhat indistinct prototype of no real scale and the same can be said of the model. It was not a good seller in 1967 but today in perfect condition is worth £150

Most of the competitors had introduced faster wheels on thinner axles. For example, Lesney had converted their miniatures in the Matchbox Series to faster running models which were known as 'Superfast'. Corgi introduced 'Whizz Wheels'. Although they continued to develop and release further highly collectable character toys through the 1970s including a larger James Bond Aston Martin and more Muppet and Magic Roundabout toys, the desirability of the range models are of significantly less interest to collectors.

However, many collectors are of the opinion that Corgi toys, and that includes post-1970 toys made up to 1983 (when Mettoy went into receivership), have great potential. Corgi toys have, with the exception of the character toys, been undervalued by collectors. For example, a new collector could amass a respectable Corgi collection within a few months at about a third of the price of a comparable Dinky toy collection. The Corgi range of toys, of which only a few have been mentioned here, were of the very highest quality. Children who bought them loved them – they were liked by the parents, too, because they lasted. Maybe this is one of the reasons why they are relatively easy to find at swapmeets and specialist collector model shops today!

In 1983 the new company of Corgi Toys was formed. The new policy of the management was to concentrate on making models aimed at collectors. Of course many of the range models continued but these new Corgi Classic cars were aimed more at adults rather than children. Production runs were in some cases as low as 5000 models. They have become very popular and are in much demand. In late 1989 Mattell (q.v.) bought out Corgi Toys and it is unclear whether this range of toys is to be continued.

· CORONATION · · COACHES ·

These can be classed as toys as the earlier coaches made in the 1930s were sold as toys to be used by children along with their armies of lead soldiers. They can also be classed as royal memorabilia because many were sold to adults as souvenirs of the coronation. They were

The most famous of all the commemorative coaches—and a beautiful example tastefully executed. Although common in 1953, these coaches have become increasingly rare and now command a value of £175 with the original box. The miniature version achieved sales of 1,000,000 in 1953 but being small and fragile could easily be lost. A mint and boxed example today is worth £75

and probably always will be a popular collectable.

DIECAST

Both Britains Ltd and John Hill Co made superb examples of the coach used in the 1937 coronation. Both companies produced large gift sets containing the coach and horses with an array of footsoldiers, Yeomen of the Guard, Guardsmen and Life Guards on horseback. Many examples of these sets have survived because when taken out of their boxes they were often carefully placed on display with the china. John Hill at one time worked for Britains and after a while launched his own company using many of the techniques he had learned from Britains. Although desirable, the John Hill Co sets are less valuable than Britains. Missing figures and horses' broken legs have a dramatic effect on value for either set. The ultimate find for a collector is a set with the figures and coach still tied onto the original unit within the box. Britains also made a coronation coach but without the escorts for the 1937 set in 1953. So popular was this item that they continued to produce it until the early 1960s.

Lesney Products (later Matchbox Toys Ltd) made two versions of the

This less well known Coronation Coach is rather more of a novelty toy than the diecast versions. This example is pre-war. Powered by a simple clockwork motor, it has a limited appeal; £50 unboxed

coach in 1952. The large-sized coach and eight horses measured some 16 inches in length and came packaged in a red box. Several hundred exist with two royal figures sitting in the coach. When it was discovered that it would be only the Queen travelling to Westminster Abbey in the coach a male figure was removed from the diecast tools. Several thousand single-figure coaches then followed. With this success, Lesney then reduced the size of the coach and made one million small coaches (4.5 inches). These are by far the most common of the well-known coaches but are quite difficult to find with the original box.

Other British diecast toy companies also made coronation coaches including one by Benbros which was a copy of the small Lesney coach (the Benbros coach has details on the coach doors) and also Morris & Stone. These coaches do not command such high prices as Britains, John Hill Co and Lesney.

Many of today's toy manufacturers have probably already designed the coach for King Charles III's coronation and they too will, no doubt, become a collectable item.

TINPLATE

The most famous toy manufacturer of coronation coaches was Taylor & Barrett of London. They produced a charming clockwork-driven coach of the 1937 coronation in tin which was highly decorated. Although toy-like in comparison to its diecast counterparts, they too have become highly regarded by collectors.

Manufacturers
Benbros (q.v.), Britains (q.v.), John Hill Co (q.v.), Lesney (q.v.), Morris & Stone (q.v.), Taylor & Barrett.

dinky

Over the past 20 years the hobby of collecting diecast model vehicles has grown from being the preserve of the eccentric few to virtually a national pastime for thousands of collectors the world over. Unlike many of the products discussed in this book the most collected range of miniatures in Britain are the products of a British company. The company's name is Meccano (q.v.) and the models are known as Dinky toys.

Dinky toys were yet another successful product from the fertile imagination of Meccano's founder, Frank Hornby. His original aim had been to produce a range of figures and vehicles which would complement the large selection of model railways his factories were successfully selling. It must have become very obvious very quickly that these new playthings had play value far in excess of even his trains and the company were very quick to realise and capitalise on this fact. The first vehicles, which included a tractor and a small lorry, were very quickly joined by a model of the *Queen Mary* and these in turn were joined by figures, dolls' house furniture, small train outfits and even aeroplanes.

World War II halted production as the company turned to the war effort, but by 1944 plans were being drawn up to produce many new models with ships, aeroplanes, cars and numerous other vehicles. In 1946 the range, which consisted of old models reissued and new models of contemporary forms of transport, was launched to a receptive market. The period from 1946 to 1964 is widely regarded as the golden age of Dinky toys from the collector's point of view. The models, especially the road-going vehicles, exuded an air of quality mainly as a result of the amount of metal used in their manufacture. The packaging was to become famous through its simple nostalgia-laden designs.

From 1964 to the end of production in 1979 the models suffered from a gradual decline in appeal. The factors which caused this were varied but it is true to state that Dinky did not invest

This 28 Series Van is cast from an almost pure lead mixture. Whilst these pre-war delivery vans can be worth up to £2,000, this example is worth £275, even in this condition

The Chrysler Airflow graphically reveals the distortion and swelling caused by metal fatigue; £50. The Tractor is unaffected by fatigue and is one of the first six vehicles made by Dinky; £200

sufficiently in the necessary machinery or even its workforce to remain truly competitive.

Corgi Toys had been launched by the Mettoy Group (q.v.) in the late 1950s and with the benefit of the latest casting techniques and the willingness to adopt a host of realistic features which added play value to their products, began to outsell Dinky, their greatest rival. Corgi Toys were more competitively priced and they were quick to capitalise on the growing market of television- and cinema-related toys – a market Dinky studiously ignored until it was almost too late. Lesney Products (q.v.), the pioneers of advanced pressure-fed castings, had effectively created a new market for their miniature vehicles but in the late 1960s started to encroach on Dinky's ground with their King Size range.

One of the advantages of collecting Dinky toys is undoubtedly that, with well over 1000 different castings to choose from, the models can be collected for very different reasons and with very different goals in mind. Listed below are some of the categories collectors may consider before finally deciding on what to collect. Accompanying them are some factors which can greatly affect the choice.

PRE-WAR MODELS

These are very hard to find today in any condition and where recognised can be expensive to buy. Prices start at about £30 for any model in poor condition. One major disadvantage of pre-war Dinky toys is the widespread existence of metal fatigue in the zinc alloy casting. Metal fatigue is a major problem to the collector and the reader should be aware that it is a non-reversible reaction caused by impurities in the alloy used in manufacture. With time, affected metal begins to expand and crack in a pattern similar to crazy paving. Its progress can be arrested by using a strong glue coating on the inside of the body and this will serve to hold the casting together but it does not prevent the fatigue. In reality, if a model is not handled too often and not subjected to the extremes of climate all may be well. However, as some models made pre-war in mint or exceptional condition can be worth £500, the implications of models breaking or crumbling need careful thought! The tyres used on these pre-war models are prone to perishing, which can either manifest itself by an appearance of a flat tyre of simply cracking or crumbling. Replacement tyres are available through specialist shops and it is generally accepted that their presence in a model does not detract from its value.

Replacement parts are also available for many pre- and post-war models and they are generally there to replace the obvious bits that were easily lost or broken. Unlike tyres, however, their presence on a model is a factor which will detract from a model's value and they are quite easily spotted: they usually have a brighter appearance than the original and are made of a white metal which is soft and can be bent by exerting a modest amount of pressure.

One factor in favour of the collector is that very thorough browsing through jumble sales and car boot sales may well provide dividends. Many of the very early issues of Dinky toys were not marked as such on their baseplates but should be marked Meccano, although this may be on an obscure part of the model so do inspect it thoroughly. The name Dinky Toys was adopted as a brand name for many of their existing models but these were not marked as such. This also applies to many of the figures available at that time as well as numerous accessories, most notably diecast trains.

As has already been stated, many of the cars were reissued after

This Rolls Royce is worth £30 unboxed. The Hillman Minx and Austin Devon are in the rare and sought-after two-tone liveries. These liveries were only found in boxes and are worth £200 each. The Riley can be found both boxed and unboxed at £100.

Only two liveries of the Morris Commercial were produced, that of the Royal Mail and that of Capstan Cigarettes. The latter is hard to find in good or mint condition and is now worth £170 boxed. The Trojan Vans are now worth £150 in boxed condition

the war but fortunately many of the vehicles bore small casting differences which help to date them accurately. The most notable feature of pre-war issues is that they have undetailed, plain diecast hubs. Those produced from 1946 have a raised circle which was cast to resemble a hub cap. This is accepted as a very good and instant means of identification. Many of the pre-war models were issued with and without tinplate chassis and each model should be inspected to ensure that its base is not missing. In general, it will also be noticed that pre-war cars and lorries were issued in much brighter and more varied colours than their post-war counterparts. It should also be noted that cars and lorries were not issued in boxes before the war, only in trade boxes of six or gift sets containing varied selections of the available models.

AEROPLANES

These form the second-largest group within the Dinky range, although the most varied and rarer items were produced before 1939. Aeroplane prices are generally not as high as those asked for cars but they are more fragile than their earthbound counterparts, mainly because the tin propellers they featured are easily bent, damaged or lost. Metal fatigue is a constant problem in Dinky aircraft and because of their less rigid shape can lead to drooping or missing sections of wings and other horrors. These problems aside, this range covers nearly all the important aircraft of the times and makes for a comprehensive display. Many of these items were unboxed but equally many were available only in gift sets. The finish on many of the early issues can vary between civilian and military guise, and many models were reissued in the early post-war years with small casting differences.

dinky

These small aircraft need to be closely examined to find the Dinky brand name. The Aircraft are worth £30 each, the Helicopter £45

During the 1950s and 1960s, Dinky produced contemporary aircraft of both military and civilian types. Fewer post-war examples were produced, however, and aircraft were not heavily featured until 1965. At that time, however, a new range was produced in a much larger scale. These large models had operating features such as motorised propellers and retractable undercarriages and were generally very well made.

SHIPS

Ships first appeared in the range in 1934 and were quickly introduced in some variety to form a comprehensive range. Unlike other ranges of Dinky toys they were all produced to a more or less constant scale of 150 feet to 1 inch and were all waterline models (they did not have keels). The majority of the subjects chosen were from the Royal Navy but the most valuable and collected are those of the civilian lines, with models such as the *Queen Mary* and the *Empress of Britain* well detailed in attractive colours.

Unfortunately for the collector Dinky did not see fit to continue the range after 1945 and except for a range of six very toy-like metal and plastic larger-scale models which appeared between 1975 and 1979, nothing of real interest was produced after the war.

CARS

It will becove obvious to the reader that in setting about forming a collection of Dinky toys it would pay to specialise in a particular area. As we have discussed above, a natural historical break presents itself at the outbreak of World War II but perhaps more important is that the individual should choose the type of model he wishes to collect. This is possible with Dinky toys because the range is so comprehensive. It is generally not sufficient to specialise in just cars, for example, as this automatically includes racing cars, record-breaking cars, television-related cars, emergency vehicles, American and European cars and even taxis. If the category of 'just cars' sounds too restricting, it should be remembered that all the cars produced before 1950 were unboxed and all came with different colours, some casting differences, different baseplates and different types of wheels. Many versions were exported in different colours to export-only markets. Listed below are some of the main categories that are commonly used in collecting together with some notes.

Passenger cars:

There are literally hundreds of castings to collect in this series which encompasses both the pre- and post-war periods. Although at first glance the Dinky numbering system seems to have no logic to it at all, it does in fact have a sequence of sorts and the first two cars ever produced are known as the 22 series. These two vehicles, a sports car and a coupé, are commonly found in orange and cream and green and yellow respectively, both being fitted with tin wheels. The next series was issued in 1935 and was a range of five saloons, together with an ambulance and a two- and four-seater tourer; several of these were actually renumbered and reissued as recognisable marques such as Rolls-Royce, Daimler and Vauxhall. Some of the 36 series were reissued after the war as were the succeeding series of 37, 38 and 39.

After the war, the production of more instantly recognisable cars went into full swing and there are many more survivors to be found today. As all Dinkys were contemporary vehicles they are quite easy to date. Windscreens and working features began to appear in the late 1950s and the wheels changed to a shiny aluminium in 1959. Dinky, however, did tend to produce cars long after the real car had been discontinued: the Riley RMB, for instance, was not phased out of production until 1960 whilst the real thing had disappeared in 1953. This period, from the war to about 1964, is regarded as the heyday of Dinky toys and certainly the most collected by today's

dinky

Four rare colour schemes on 1950s Dinkys. Cars such as these, particularly with two-tone colours, are worth £250 each if in boxed condition

Guy Lorries have always been expensive, this Weetabix version is worth £1,500, the Lyons Swiss Roll £1,200 boxed

All of the Foden 8 Wheel Lorries are extremely sought after and have soared in value over the last few years. Even the extremely battered and scratched survivors are worth at least £35. Superb examples such as these command £300 for the first series cab type, and £400 for the unusual red and green version boxed

collectors. Models from this period have a simple charm and were
finished in shades of colour very redolent of their time. This was
before the era of metallic paint and so these models are coloured in
the deep flat shades of the day, not, it should be noted, always with
great realism. Dinky would be very quick to rejuvenate sales of
ageing vehicles with new liveries, often in two-tone colours. These
two-toned vehicles are in great demand today as they were
produced in fewer quantities than the previous single colour
schemes.

In the 1960s, faced with stiff competition from Corgi (q.v.),
Matchbox (q.v.) and Spot-On, Dinky reacted by fitting innovations
such as opening doors, boots and bonnets to their models. Fingertip
steering was added to certain new models. Ironically, it is features
such as these which began to tell against their collectability. Dinky
were not adept at making such features realistic. Some examples
include the MGB with opening doors which has unsightly gaps
around the door edges; the Jaguar 3.4 has a very narrow wheel
track, and the Silver Cloud Mark III which had five opening parts
is full of unsightly gaps. These models from the early 1960s attract
less than half the price of their 1950s forerunners in perfect
condition.

As the 1960s moved into the 1970s such features as metallic paint
and new standardised 'speed wheels' became commonplace. These
are even less liked by collectors as the accent was removed from
realism and towards play value. For example, the NSU RO80 had
luminous plastic seats in 1971. Standards fell steadily through this
decade and by the end of production in 1979 the models were of
little interest to collectors.

DINKY SUPERTOYS

This second category of the brand was introduced to cover all the
larger models produced and naturally was applied to the larger
lorries. There are, however, many exceptions and Meccano appear
to have been confused with their own descriptions as some series of
model were both promoted and later demoted in and out of this
range.

The most common and most collected Supertoys are the eight-
wheeled Fodens and Leyland Octopuses produced from 1947 to
1969. These appeared in many variants of body style including
high-sided, chain-backed, tailboarded and flat-bedded varieties.
The really important factor in determining value is, however, colour
scheme. No real records exist from the factory but very rare colour
schemes can command a price of £1600–£2000 in certain cases.
With the Foden trucks, which came in two cab types, anything
which features yellow is valuable. With the Leylands the chain
variant is a very valuable and rare piece.

dinky

The new Dinky toys made by Matchbox have proved exceptionally popular and are excellent value at £6.99

Both these chassis were also produced in a tanker version but in only four liveries of petrol companies. These very attractive models have risen steadily in recent years and any good example can fetch £100 even without its original box.

In general terms, the Supertoy range was not so prolific as the cars but, as the reader will now suspect, rarity equals cost. Several Dinky Supertoys were so successful that even today they remain quite common. For this reason alone the novice collector should be wary of paying too much. Number 982, the Dinky Toys Car Transporter, was in production from 1952 to 1962 and must have been a runaway success, so much so that even today a mint and boxed standard example would not exceed £80. Further examples of common Supertoys at reasonable prices include the 972 Coles 20-Ton Crane Truck, a magnificent model yet available for £60 at the most. Unusual or even unlikely Supertoys include the 964 Elevator Loader, startlingly ugly at about £40 in perfect condition.

MILITARY MODELS

This comprehensive range has many advantages to the would-be collector. The range, especially during the years 1947 to 1964, was produced in large quantities and consequently these models are readily available today at reasonable prices. They are not as attractive as their civilian counterparts, no doubt due to their uniform colour, and this adds to the reasonable prices. Army vehicles span both Dinky and the Supertoy series and first appeared in 1933 as one of the original six models.

The most famous model in the series is the 698 Tank Transporter Set produced from 1958 to 1962; it can usually be found for about £60 in perfect condition. Very rare models such as the United Nations livery decorating an Austin Champ can reach £200 if in perfect condition.

VANS WITH ADVERTISING

This type of vehicle was always a significant part of the Dinky range both pre- and post-war. Pre-war the range consisted of the 25 series of commercial vehicles which included a range of petrol tankers and covered wagons, many of which were decorated with contemporary liveries. The 28 series consisted of 13 different liveries on three different castings. The liveries appeared simultaneously on all three castings but the casting came in order, i.e. 28/1, 2 and 3.

Post-war vans were far less numerous but are nonetheless much sought after. One of the most attractive is the No. 465 Morris van in the livery of Capstan cigarettes. Other models include a series of six liveries on a Trojan van, three on an Austin and a further three on a Bedford. An updated Bedford was introduced in 1972 to which a whole range of liveries was added, and these are well worth collecting for the future.

THE DINKY COLLECTION BY MATCHBOX

In 1987 the Dinky range was relaunched by Matchbox Toys (q.v.), who had bought the rights to the name. The new products, which did not use any parts or castings from the old range, proved to be a great success with both the public and the collectors. The models are a perfect mixture of realism and quality at an affordable price. They will prove to be a very collectable range.

· DISNEYANIA ·

When Walt Disney created Mickey Mouse in the early 1930s he probably did not consider the following that many of his film characters would create. Toys featuring Walt Disney film characters are highly collected, not only by Disney enthusiasts but also by collectors of character, battery or novelty models. Toys featuring Mickey Mouse and Goofy are by far the most popular, closely followed by Snow White and the Seven Dwarfs. Most of the common metals or materials have been used over the years.

One overriding factor affects the price of Disney-related items and that is because most toy collectors stick to a common collecting theme such as cars, boats or lead soldiers, Disney items tend to appeal to collectors across their chosen range. Thus the Britains 'Snow White' set appeals to collectors of Britains products, to collectors of lead soldiers, character toy collectors and to Disney collectors. This effectively doubles or triples the number of

This famous cartoon group dates from 1938 and is eagerly sought after by Disney, figure and TV related toy collectors. This unboxed set is worth £150

This excellent small series of famous cartoon figures was made by Lesney c 1980. They are rare in boxed condition because of the user-unfriendly packaging (they could not be repacked once opened) and so are worth £10 each but rapidly appreciating and worth collecting

collectors who would wish to buy such a set and this naturally increases the demand and therefore the price.

Cardboard: There are many examples of games made from card such as the one featured in a simple shooting gallery game featuring the Seven Dwarfs. This was made under licence in the 1950s. It would be of even greater value to the Disneyania collector if it also showed Snow White.

Plastic: This was used to make large-sized Walt Disney figures such as the toy of Mickey Mouse made from a combination of plastic and cloth. Most of the other now famous characters have been seen including Donald Duck and Minnie Mouse. Such toys are also sought after by doll collectors and general Disneyania collectors, often not as their main collecting theme but more as an ancillary prop to their display.

Diecast: several British diecast toy companies made Walt Disney figures during the 1950s. It is unclear whether they did this under licence as in many cases the toys were made with the manufacturer's trademark. Due to their crudeness and age they have a charm

d

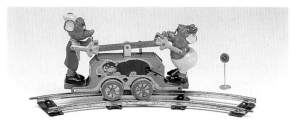

This charming cartoon character set of Gus and Jag is one of the most collectable pieces ever to be made by Brimtoy. Officially licensed from Disney and dated about 1955, it is worth £275

This model and display stand is linked to the film *20,000 Leagues Under the Sea*. Not as rare as one might expect but in this case still worth £100

that appeals to the enthusiast. Matchbox Toys (q.v.) made a range of diecast Walt Disney figures riding in Matchbox miniature cars. Models were made in 1979 through to 1980 (they also made three Popeye figures). They can still be found for sale in shops today for under £1 but are worth at least five times this price to a collector.

Lead: Britains Ltd manufactured a Snow White and the Seven Dwarfs set in 1939 and continued to make the set for several years after World War II. Complete sets, especially in their original box, are quite scarce. Such has been the popularity of this set that copies have been made not in lead but in white metal. It has proved difficult to simulate the aged colours of the originals and modern-day copies are too bright.

Tin: Too many examples to list but do look out for clockwork-driven and battery-operated toys such as Mickey Mouse riding a bicycle or the many tinplate clockwork Pinocchio toys made by the Louis Marx Co in the immediate pre-World War II period. During the 1940s British manufacturers made many different examples of children's table placings: cups and saucers, teapots and plates all featuring Walt Disney characters. During the 1950s Brimtoy (Wells) (q.v.) of London made beautiful tracked sets featuring characters from many Walt Disney films. The track and engine bodies were all made from tin but the figures were made from a composition material. Walt Disney figures that have been seen include Mickey and Minnie Mouse and the two little mice, Gus and Jaq from Cinderella. Disney toys will, of course, be of interest to other groups of collectors. One example is the metal clockwork 'Nautilus' submarine made by the Sutcliffe company. This was based on the submarine used in the film *20,000 Leagues Under the Sea* released in the early 1960s. Such was the popularity of the toy that it continued in production until the late 1970s. This toy would be of interest to not only Disney enthusiasts but also character toy and boat collectors.

Disney toys are made to this day and although there are thousands to collect they do make a colourful and interesting collection.

Manufacturers
Britains (q.v.), Marx (q.v.), Matchbox (q.v.).

This simple toy of the dwarf characters is of less value because it is merely a variation on a theme – a shooting gallery could be made using any subject matter; £40

d

· DOLLS ·
· (1860–1925) ·

It is amazing just how many dolls from the 19th and early 20th centuries have survived. They were often bought for the children of upper and middle classes, or as leaving presents for nannies and governesses. Victorian children, we are told, had a more strict upbringing than children of today, and so were encouraged to look after their dolls. Girls also seem to have a less destructive attitude to their toys compared to boys and this may be a factor why so few trains, boats and similar 'boy' toys from the 1900s have survived intact.

This early German 'Pumpkin' Headed Doll is made from wax over composition material and dates from 1860. The wax has become brittle and cracked with age which accounts for its rather dour expression; c £175

WAX DOLLS

Various materials have been used over the years to make dolls' heads and bodies. These include wood, papier-mâché and wax. Wax dolls were made as long ago as the days of the Roman Empire and continued to be made until the beginning of the century. Wax dolls were prolific during the 19th century and can be classified in two ways:

Wax doll: Layers of wax were poured into a mould. Each layer was allowed to cool before the next layer was added, resulting in a dolls's head made entirely of wax. These are not common. Various substances were added to the inside of the doll's head such as paste, glue, sawdust, plaster or resin as a strengthening exercise.

Waxed doll: Wood, porcelain, rag, rubber and papier-mâché have been coated with wax to improve the appearance of the doll's head. In most cases the head was dipped into a bath of hot wax and when withdrawn was allowed to cool. On early waxed dolls, the features such as cheeks and lips were painted on the face before the head was dipped. Later these facial features were painted onto the wax itself.

Both types of wax doll had non-wax bodies. Usually the bodies were made from cloth filled with sawdust or straw and in some cases leather was used to form the arms and legs. It was an expensive process to give wax dolls hair – for wax dolls the hair was inserted in small groups, whereas for waxed dolls a hole was cut in the head and hair was then inserted into this slit.

Both types of wax doll are easily damaged by changes in temperature and many surviving examples have very cracked faces. It is not uncommon to find wax dolls missing their wax eyes – these would have popped out when the face got too warm!

Few wax dolls have manufacturers' marks and so they often prove difficult to date. However, good quality wax dolls were made by Pierottis between 1860 and 1930. In Germany, Kammer & Reinhardt also made good quality wax dolls. Waxed dolls were made in a variety of countries including the USA, France, England and Austria.

CHINA DOLLS

China-headed dolls made of glazed porcelain were most popular during Queen Victoria's reign. Generally it was only the head or limbs (known as china limb dolls) that were made in glazed porcelain, the doll's cotton body being stuffed or made from wood in the shape of a peg or a combination of both. The heads often had a flat bottom with holes which then fitted over the peg or could be attached to the body. Few heads were stamped with a manufacturer's mark and the only way to identify them is from specialist bodies or from original

This Bisque Headed Doll dates from the early 1900s and was made by Limage's; £150

d

A South Sea Island Baby also dates from the turn of the century and being coloured is rather more unusual. Actually used by a firm of German travel agents to promote their holidays; £150

catalogues. However, as a general guide a head with four holes signifies German origin, whereas eight holes signifies French origin. A typical Victorian glazed porcelain doll would have short black hair reflecting the fashion of the 1840s to 1860s and set blue eyes. Much rarer would be a doll with swivel neck, painted brown eyes, pierced ears and a bald head to accommodate a wig. A fine china-headed doll should have a detailed face and high quality painted features such as eyes, nostrils, eyebrows and hair. The poorer quality dolls usually lack the red dot in the corner of the eye and the red line above the eye. Although most china-headed dolls were finished with black painted hair, it was more common after 1888 to find fair or blonde hair. Although china-headed dolls continued to be made during the early part of this century, they do not have the same feel or charm as the old ones. The latter often had casting imperfections, ingrained dirt from the less sophisticated kilns and a poorer texture and colour from the paint used.

The size of china-limbed dolls varied from 2 inches up to just under 3 feet. The smaller dolls were often made as miniature dolls for dolls' houses and are very collectable.

During the 1860s a new form of china-headed doll was developed. Instead of using a glazed porcelain, ceramic manufacturers discovered that bisque, which was a ceramic material with a non-glossy hard surface, could be used successfully to make dolls. Bisque heads could be either pressed or poured into a mould. The former were usually rough on the inside of the head and were generally made prior to 1890. Before 1880 most bisque heads were the shoulder type and many of these had moulded hair and sometimes moulded hats. Known as blonde bisque dolls to differentiate them from later bisque dolls, they closely resemble glazed porcelain dolls both in the construction of their bodies, i.e. a stuffed cloth body, and the shape and design of the head. These blonde bisques were also popular as dolls' house miniatures.

Bisque dolls were produced mainly in France and Germany. Unlike the blonde bisques the later bisque dolls fitted with glass eyes would have their crowns sliced away to be replaced with a cork pate on French dolls and a cardboard or plaster pate on German dolls. The most famous French bisque dolls are those made by Jumeau, Bru, Limage and by the doll federation of France – the Société de Fabrication des Bébés et Jouets (SFBJ).

This beautiful doll was made by Simon & Halbig in the early 1900s. The clothes are original and the maker's name is clearly visible on the back of the head; £250

Jumeau

Founded by Pierre Jumeau in 1842 and carried on by Emile Jumeau until 1899, at which time the company became a part of the SFBJ, Jumeau bisque dolls gained international recognition during the mid-1850s more for their clothes than the quality of their heads.

This doll with 'tremble tongue' was made by Goebel in the 1900s. It still wears its original clothes; £300

However, by the 1880s they were regarded as being in the same class as their greatest rival, Bru. Characteristics of Jumeau dolls are very large eyes. Features of Jumeau dolls include talking bébé dolls using voice boxes; some dolls could say 'mama' or 'papa' depending on which string was pulled; bébé dolls with flirting eyes, counterweighted sleeping eyes, closed and opened mouths and walking mechanisms. Jumeau heads were fixed to bodies made from both composition and leather. In July 1987, a Jumeau doll dated around 1894 dressed as a Russian sailor with the capband and the Russian Imperial Cypher from one of the royal family's yachts, sold for £6600 at Christie's Auction House in London. The name Jumeau can usually be found incised or stamped on the body or the head as well as 'Médaille d'or 1878' (a reference to one of the many awards received by the Jumeau firm).

Bru

Founded in 1866 in Paris, France, and traded under the Bru trademark until 1899 when, like Jumeau, it amalgamated into the SFBJ. Bru bisque dolls are some of the most sought after today and were well known for their high quality. Both dressed and undressed dolls were made and many were exported to the USA. Always in direct competition to Jumeau, the Bru family were continually upgrading the play value of their dolls and by 1867 had developed a crying doll and even a double-faced doll.

Max Hand Werk c 1920s—a partially reclothed but still collectable example; £200

· GOLLIWOG ·

The Golliwog (also spelt Gollywog) rag doll character was devised in 1895 by Miss F. Upton, an American lady who illustrated and published children's books. The idea was taken up by several rag doll manufacturers who realised that the character was well liked by children. Enid Blyton used a Golliwog character in many of her Noddy and Big Ears stories. Golliwog dolls are still being made today and have become very collectable.

Manufacturers
Deans Rag Book Co.

Now thought of as a relic from a less enlightened age, golliwogs can be classed as curios. This one dates from the 1950s and was made by Wendy Boston. All golliwogs are composed of soft material and are not found with moulded heads; £35

· JACK · IN · · THE · BOX ·

The original concept of a toy that sprang out of a box was developed during the 16th century. Many of the characters used were taken from children's nursery rhymes or folklore. Not only could the Jack in the Box delight, it could also frighten, and the use of Punch and Judy figures during the 19th century was common. Jack in the Boxes continue to be made today by both the smaller traditional toy makers and the larger manufacturers such as Fisher Price.

As time passes various manufacturers have updated the 'Jack' figure. The Tom and Jerry figure is a typical example. Jack in the Box toys are collected today but as a specialist subject, it should not be difficult to find them at jumble sales and car boot sales for nominal prices. *See also: Character; Disneyania.*

Manufacturers
Fisher Price, Marx (q.v.), Mettoy (q.v.).

These toys constitute a specialised form of collecting but this particular example can also fall into the category of character toys, having been licensed from the copyright holders of Tom and Jerry c 1970; £70

matchbox

The firm of Lesney Products (q.v.) was formed by three partners in the late 1940s. Although one of them, Rodney Smith, was to leave in 1950 the other two, Leslie Smith and Jack Odell, went on to establish one of the most prestigious diecast toy companies in the world. Many people remember, or may have stored away in one of their now grown-up children's toy boxes, a selection of the Matchbox Miniature models first made in 1953. Known as pocket-money toys, these beautifully-made toys from the Matchbox Series are just one of the many ranges made by Lesney. The more significant and well-known ranges are outlined below.

THE EARLY LESNEY TOYS

A range of 15 large-sized models (similar in size to Dinky toys) which began in 1948 with road-building equipment such as a Road Roller, Cement Mixer and Bulldozer. The Road Roller was very similar to the Dinky equivalent but the Lesney toy was never issued with a baseplate. Few of these early toys ever referred to Lesney and will only be identified as such by Matchbox enthusiasts. Lesney added two horse-drawn vehicles in 1949 – the Rag and Bone Cart and the Milk Cart. The latter toy was scaled down in 1953 and issued as No. 7 in the Matchbox Series. The Rag and Bone Cart was issued with seven pieces of unpainted junk, a painted driver and a painted horse. Such a model is seldom seen for sale. In mint and boxed condition the asking price is usually in excess of £2000. The majority of these carts were painted in yellow, but an even rarer find is a cart painted in mid-green. Other now-famous early Lesney toys include both the small and large-sized 1953 Coronation Coaches (q.v.) and the Muffin the Mule Puppet (see Character Toys). With the exception of the Coronation Coaches, any one of these toys in any state will be of interest to a Matchbox collector. The coaches will usually be found in mint

These very early, quite crude and obscure products from Lesney in the late 1940s are in fact often unrecognised by toy dealers. They are very valuable and sought after by specialists. Cement Mixer: £90; Prime Mover: £500 boxed; Milk Float: £450 boxed

First Series Yesteryears are amongst the most collected of all early diecast vehicles, with thousands of interested collectors. Such is the demand for these superb miniatures, that prices remain high at about £80 on average for these boxed examples, which have appreciated steadily over the years

condition as they were always intended to be an ornament or souvenir rather than a toy. Obviously, the better the condition the more valuable it will be, but examples of very distressed early Lesney toys missing paint and parts will still fetch a surprisingly high value if the seller knows what he has.

THE MATCHBOX SERIES
– REGULAR WHEELS

This range was introduced by Lesney in 1953. The large-sized Road Roller had been successfully scaled down and it was decided by Lesney to make an extensive range of 75 miniature diecast models that were so small that they could almost fit into a matchbox. The range was contemporary in that the Lesney management chose vehicles that were easily identifiable and were in most cases being driven on the roads at the time of their introduction. They now evoke great nostalgia of the 1950s and 1960s, and are eagerly sought after by not only Matchbox enthusiasts but also collectors of classic cars. Examples include the Jaguar 3.8 (issued in 1962), Morris Minor 1000 (issued in 1958) or the Aston Martin DB2-4 Mark I (issued in 1958) to name a few. Most models were issued several times over a protracted period of time – these colour variations are much in demand today as inevitably the shorter time the model was available in a certain colour the harder it will be to find. All models were fitted with relatively thick axles and metal wheels which in time were changed to plastic wheels. Parents developed a liking for the Matchbox Series because unlike Dinky toys children could not remove the Lesney wheels. They were always given at least two coats of paint and were designed to withstand most of the abuse that a child was likely to give them.

These early examples from the Matchbox 1-75 series are easy to display, possess great charm and are much sought after. These mint and boxed examples date from the late 1950s and are worth £25, £35, £45, £35 and £20

Yesteryear Commercial Vans—The 'Goblin' livery with a light grey roof was a short run in 1988 and is worth £15. The Arnotts and Sunlight Soap liveries were produced in extremely small quantities for various reasons, and so demand exceeds supply. In 1981, when they first appeared, they cost £5 each, but are now worth £140 each. The Coca-Cola is not quite so rare and is worth £45

A trend in recent years is for many hitherto non-Matchbox collectors to take up building a Matchbox Series collection. For example, collectors of Dinky toys may have completed their Dinky collection or may be just looking for one or two rare models and so to keep their interest in the hobby alive have changed direction to Matchbox. With the exception of the rare models, collectors expect the models to be in mint and boxed condition. Due to their size, the smallest paint defect could render the model undesirable! The range is vast (1953–69) and this has led many collectors to specialise within the series. For example, some only collect first edition

Second Series boxed Yesteryears such as these are also avidly and widely collected but are easier to find. The result of wider availability is reflected in the value at £35 with the exception of the Fire Engine which is worth £125 boxed

These three examples are standard issues but with very rare colour schemes. To a collector they are worth £175 for the two-tone green Mercedes Benz boxed and £275 for the slightly less common Bentley and Lagonda (centre)

models in their first issued liveries. Others may collect the whole range but may not be too interested in the boxes or the colour types. The collector who chooses to forgo the necessity of boxes can in many cases save up to 50 per cent, i.e. a mint boxed Miniature usually sells for double the price of the same model without its box.

MODELS OF YESTERYEAR

This series of vintage, sports and classic cars, trucks, trains and steam-driven vehicles was first released in 1956. They were about twice the size of the early Matchbox Series miniatures and were of

matchbox

immediate interest to railway model enthusiasts. Many an example of the first model in the range, the Y1 Allchin Traction Engine, has been found repainted by such an enthusiast! It has been estimated by Matchbox that at any given time there are some 100,000 Models of Yesteryear collectors throughout the world. Some will only collect certain categories from the series, e.g. racing cars or commercial vans. The range is still being made today and has grown from the original 16 (made by 1960) up to over 35 different models or liveries at any one time (1990) as part of the range.

THE FIRST SERIES YESTERYEARS

These were made between 1956 and 1963 and in mint boxed condition are much in demand today, with prices for a standard model in excess of £50. Variations to the shade or colour of the paint can dramatically alter the value of the model. For example, the Y6 lorry with Osram livery in dark grey is worth £150 as compared to the more common light grey version (£100).

As a model was deleted it was replaced with a new model, e.g. a second series model and so on. One of the most famous second series models is the Y4 Shand Mason Fire Engine which was issued with three detachable plastic firemen, which have with time often gone missing. It should be noted that replacement firemen made from white metal can be obtained from specialist shops. These were not made by Lesney and do not add any monetary value to an otherwise mint model.

COMMERCIAL VANS

This category is most popular with Models of Yesteryear collectors. With few exceptions Lesney, and in later years Matchbox Toys Ltd, issued several liveries on the same basic model. For example, the Y12 Ford Model 'T' Van featured 18 different liveries from its inception in 1979 until its demise in 1988. Although most of them can be bought today at an average price of £6, some of them are quite expensive due to very limited production runs or being regional issues only. One of the most famous Y12 models is the Arnott's Biscuits van issued for the Australian market only. It was also released just as Lesney was going into receivership and the new Matchbox Toys Ltd management prematurely ceased its production so that in total only 18,000 models were released. Within weeks of its issue, Arnott's models were being imported back into the UK and selling for £10 (three times their normal selling price). Today an Arnott's van can be seen for sale in the price range of between £125–£150! Other commercial vans such as the Y5 Talbot van – first issued in 1979 – are still being produced in 1990. The most famous Y5 van is undoubtedly that of the Lipton's Tea livery with the Royal Crest. Lesney were told in no uncertain terms by the

Lord Chamberlain's office that they were breaking the law by using the crest. The Lipton's livery was then modified. Many collectors must have heard about the mix-up because most of the Royal Crest models were bought up quickly. This was pure speculation on the part of the collector. Within weeks there was a premium to pay for the model – the selling price was between £12 and £15. However, this is still the same price today for the model because since 1979 many of these speculative models have flooded the market! In 1988 Matchbox released a new model, the Y12 GMC van with a Goblin Vacuum Cleaner livery. The first 6000 models were fitted with grey roofs. The Quality Assurance Management stopped the production because they were not happy with the finish of paint. The roof was then changed to black. This small run of grey-roofed Goblin vans was in the main sent to the UK shops and when discovered created a lot of interest. Consequently, when the facts and figures had been confirmed by collectors, the model price jumped overnight to £12– £15.

SALOON CARS

This aspect of the range attracts the collector whose other hobbies may be centred around the actual vehicles. The Yesteryear range can be a cheap and easy way in which to build up a vintage transport display. One of the most famous Models of Yesteryear saloons is undoubtedly the Y4 1930 Duesenberg car issued in 1976 in the colour scheme of white body, red chassis and wings and yellow plastic hood and seats. A mix-up between the production line and the management enabled just over 100 such models to be boxed up with the standard model which was finished in metallic red with black hood and seats. All the models were distributed throughout the known Lesney markets. Obviously many were played with by children and it is estimated that no more than 20 such models have survived. At auction one of these rare Yesteryear models would attract a price well in excess of £1000.

Finally, with regard to the current range of Models of Yesteryear, some potential collectors may be put off by the fact that the range subjects are becoming obscure, i.e. models of 1930s classic cars made in the 1960s by Lesney may have been seen on the roads or would certainly have been recognised but the same cannot be said of 1920s steam-driven vehicles made in 1990 by Matchbox! They do, however, make an attractive display and are relatively cheap to buy.

MATCHBOX DINKY

Matchbox Toys acquired the defunct brandname Dinky (q.v.) in 1987. As a collectable range of well-made diecast miniature vehicles, the Dinky collection is already a winner. The subject

matchbox

matter includes classic cars such as the 'E' Type Jaguar, the MGB GT and the Volkswagen Beetle. Matchbox issued their first Dinky in early 1989 and had released ten different models by the end of that year. Their aim is to make a range of cars, vans and lorries from the 1950s and 1960s. Whereas younger generations may find it hard to identify with some of the more obscure subject matters found in the Models of Yesteryear range, this should not be the case with Dinky.

SUPERFAST

When the wheels and axles on the Miniatures range of Matchbox Series models were upgraded in 1968/9 the name of the range was changed to 'Superfast'. There have been thousands of different Superfast models made since 1969. The present-day Miniatures range is no longer referred to as Superfast; instead they are known as Matchbox Miniatures. The 1990 range is on sale at most toy and hobby shops priced usually at less than £1. The earlier Superfast models in mint and boxed condition can often be found in obsolete toy shops or at toy fairs priced between £3 and £5. Although space may be a problem, a new collector can build up a large collection quickly for a small financial outlay.

Four models from the 1970s series of Matchbox miniatures with 'Superfast' low friction axles. Objects of desire to a small but growing band of collectors, they may well be attractive to the collector in the future; £4 each

·MECCANO·

See Dinky; Constructor Kits.

·METTOY·

The first Mettoy catalogue was published in 1936 showing a large range of tinplate/pressed metal toys similar to many of their earlier Tipp Co (q.v.) toys. The majority had clockwork mechanisms. Some of the more desirable pre-war Mettoy products include the large racing car finished in red and white and the medium-sized saloon car and caravan. The range included fire engines, road rollers, motorcycles and aeroplanes. Although unsophisticated compared with many of the aeroplanes being made during the 1930s in Germany, they do have a charm of their own and being relatively inexpensive to buy today are quite collectable.

Although toy production continued until 1942, the shortage of raw material caused by the war effort forced the company to cease production. Instead the company turned their skills to making armaments.

In 1946 a new catalogue was published. This combined many of the toys made before the war. One way in which to reduce origination costs was to make slight modifications to the tools of

This Saloon Car and Caravan which looks pre-war is in fact from 1946— a reflection on the lack of development of new toys as a result of the war. Not that rare in collecting circles as a dealer found a warehouse full of these in 1986; £95

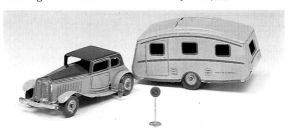

m

One of the last traditional toys made from tinplate, this Fire Engine must have looked distinctly old fashioned even when new in 1954; £90. In contrast this very heavily cast Mechanical Racer from the same company was virtually indestructible in 1949; £40

a popular subject and so cleverly extend the range. For example, all lorries were made with the same cab but with an array of highly coloured containers or low-sided bodies.

In 1948 Mettoy released a range of the 'heavy cast' toys which were made exclusively for the Marks & Spencer stores. Gone were the unsightly 'tabs' needed to hold the pressed tin toys together. This new range was much more robust and included coaches, saloons, a fire engine, a lorry, a van and a racing car. The No. 830 mechanical racer was similar in design to Schuco racing cars and featured a clockwork engine, brake lever and all with steering wheel control! The Heavy Car Mechanical Toys range lasted until 1951. They were originally sold unboxed but under the brand name of Castoys they were also sold in boxes.

A new factory was built for Mettoy in Swansea and opened in 1949. It was from there that the famous Corgi range of diecast models would be made in the mid-1950s. However, pressed tin toys continued to be the main product – a range of inexpensive train sets were added to the range and although they are beautifully decorated do not command high prices when offered for sale today. By 1960 the last of the tin toys had been made. Production had switched entirely to diecast with all production capacity being devoted to Corgi products.

Tinplate toys are regarded as being at the cheap end of the range. Due to their robustness many have survived intact. *See also: Corgi; Tipp Co; tinplate and diecast cars; Mettoy Company.*

· MINIC ·
PRE-WAR

Tri-ang Minic became one of the best-known ranges of tinplate clockwork vehicles made by the Lines Bros. group in the ever-popular 'O' Gauge scale. They were first released in 1935. In recent years they have become highly sought after and as a consequence their prices have become somewhat high. The range has always been popular with 'O' Gauge train collectors

These Minic cars appeal greatly to collectors of tinplate as they are small, nostalgic and easy to display. Prices have risen greatly after a long period of neglect; £100 each

and enthusiasts as they add an extra dimension to a railway layout. As tinplate toys in general have become more and more expensive, many tinplate collectors have turned to Minic which not so many years ago were relatively easy to find and, just as important, were good value for money. They would not be of much use to a true classic or vintage car enthusiast as they were painted in very bright colours, and much use was made of shiny nickel-plated tin. For the fortunate collector who already has a collection of Minic they are most impressive to look at and exude the feel and nostalgia of Britain in the pre-war and early post-war eras.

Pre-war models include limousines, sports saloons, delivery lorries and buses. The Minic catalogue described the models in very general terms as they were not attempting to make exact replicas of road-going vehicles. Pre-war Minics can be identified not only from catalogues but just as easily by examining the model. For example, all early pre-war models were fitted with

The bus and jeep are two further examples of the Minic range. Buses are a particularly sought after vehicle group which command a premium over cars. The jeep is worth £75 and the bus £120. The Riley (centre) was an ill-fated attempt to continue the range into the age of plastic. Unloved, these crude models are really only of novelty value; £20

white tyres, later pre-war models as with post-war models had black tyres. However, all pre-war models were fitted with tinplate wheels/hubs, whereas post-war Minics featured diecast wheels. Most of the pre-war Minic saloons were fitted with a windscreen and dashboard made as one component. Very rare today are the pre-war cars fitted with lead passengers. Most of these early Minics had room for a battery which in turn powered the headlights or, in the case of the breakdown lorry, the gears and winch of the crane unit.

Production of Minics carried on until 1940. The mood of war was reflected in some of the models. Camouflage paint schemes were often used instead of the standard bright colours, the nickel plating was painted and lorry canopies were finished in browns and greens. The Minic range was reintroduced in 1947.

POST-WAR

Although many of the pre-war models were reissued after World War II, some of the little extras, fitted to pre-war models as standard, were dispensed with, e.g. many of the pre-war vehicles were fitted with a small red-and-yellow Shell petrol can, and the luggage racks that added a little realism were removed. A numberplate – LBL (Lines Bros. Ltd) 194 – replaced the luggage rack. These are all further aids to dating a Minic vehicle that the reader may already own. The post-war range included many of the pre-war classics – articulated lorries carrying loads such as real wooden logs (trees), planks, wooden cases and wooden barrels. However, there were more cost-saving exercises expedited. For example, compare a pre-war Minic Ambulance with a post-war version. The earlier ambulance had electric lights and a solid brass bell. On the later model the lights were non-operational and the bell had been hollowed out! Even so, early postwar Minics are just as desirable as prewar Minics and, unfortunately for the new collector, pose a considerable financial burden.

Tri-ang augmented the Minic range with a varied selection of accessories including Minic Garages and Service Stations. These will add an extra display dimension to any Minic collection and are readily sought by collectors. Many of these buildings were issued with detachable petrol pumps and oil stands. If these are missing the value of the accessory is reduced. The original box will often list the original contents, so check it all before making a purchase.

During the mid-1950s Minic tinplate models were also fitted with friction motors instead of clockwork. This range was marketed as 'Push and Go' and included examples such as the Ambulance, Dust Cart and Transport Van. 'Push and Go' vehicles are the least desirable of the Tri-ang Minic 'O' Gauge range. Prices for a mint boxed example vary between £25 and £35. This is, however, a good sub-range to start collecting because with time the pre-war and post-war clockwork Minics will price themselves beyond the reach of many collectors.

In 1951 a new series of larger-sized models made from steel were introduced in the Tri-ang Minic range. These were fitted with Push and Go mechanisms and included a 13-inch Petrol Tanker and a 14-inch Removal Van. They were ingenious toys and must have given much pleasure to the children of the time. For example, the Heavy Duty Crash Truck came with manually operated controls and an

This large-scale Removal Van, sold under the brand name Minic, was an attempt to produce a toy suitable for outside use. The heavy duty construction should have prompted larger sales than they actually achieved and so survivors in good condition are rare today. Dating from 1951 this example is worth £45

electric spotlight. This series as a whole has not been eagerly sought after as yet by collectors. They are very reasonably priced today – a mint boxed example of the Crash Truck would be in the region of £40. However, specialist collectors of petrol companies such as Shell/BP would probably pay up to £75 for the large Shell Tanker.

Tri-ang also produced a large range of Minics in 1947 made from plastic. They were made at the Lines Bros. (q.v.) factory in Merton by International Model Aircraft Ltd (who made the Frog range of aeroplanes) and were originally marketed as being 'Penguin' toys. An early example of this brand is the Riley Saloon R.M.E or R.M.F. Saloon, which is of little interest to the diehard Minic collector but would be of interest to a Riley car enthusiast. Such a toy would be valued at no more than £15. The Penguin range was quickly built up to include a Jaguar XK120 and a Buick. The Penguin brand name was abandoned in 1948. More plastic models were introduced and these along with the Penguin models were marketed as being part of the Tri-ang Minic range. Several scales were used with the smallest being OO Guage. Possibly the most attractive van in this series was the

Macleans Toothpaste van in pale blue
fitted with a replica of a tube of
toothpaste. This has been seen for sale
at £85. Large plastic cars resembling
American taxis, sports cars fitted with
horns and even a musical car were all
made during this period.

The plastic models which for so long
have been scorned by collectors have
seen an upsurge in popularity. They are
cheap to buy – at the moment many are
seen for sale in toy fairs and specialist
toy shops at no more than £15. They
have a charm of their own and being
inexpensive will enable a collector to
build up a substantial collection quite
quickly.

TRI-ANG MINIC SHIPS

This excellent range of diecast model
ships was introduced in 1959. Unlike
their great rivals Meccano Dinky whose
models had wheels, the Minic ships,
although being more realistic, had less
play value. The range was ended in
1964. The range of Minic ships is
expensive and includes ocean liners
such as the RMS *Aquitania* and Royal
Naval ships such as HMS *Bulwark*.
Tri-ang also produced Harbour Sets and
presentation sets. Together they make a
superb display and are seen for sale at

Minic diecast ships are the
only serious alternative to
the Dinky variety available
to the collector. These
examples date from the
late 1950s. Minic ships and
accessories can form a
most impressive collection;
£25 each

most of the good toy fairs. Some dealers specialise in just this range and prices are generally fair, although mint and boxed examples do command a premium. Many of these models were fitted with masts and invariably with time these have gone missing. In general terms the ocean liners are more valuable than the naval ships. It should be noted that many of the ships were reissued in 1976, all fitted with wheels that did little or nothing for the collectors. This 'second series' of Minic ships are not expensive and are not as desirable as the 'first series'.

· MONEY · BOXES ·
See Banks

· MOTORCYCLES ·
TINPLATE

The earliest toy motorcycles date back to just before World War I. Toy manufacturers such as Lehmann (q.v.) made a series of tinplate clockwork motorcycles with riders during the 1920s which are now worth thousands of pounds and beyond the scope of this book. However, toys made during the 1930s can still be found and can be worth hundreds of pounds. The Germans made the majority of tinplate clockwork motorcycles, but Mettoy also made good quality toys during the 1940s and 1950s.

After World War II the Japanese replaced the Germans as being the leading tin toy manufacturing country. During the 1960s they introduced many examples of battery-operated motorcycles or simpler friction-powered toys. Many of the Japanese motorcycles were more accurate representations of real bikes and used easily identifiable

The MAC700 Cyclist is widely regarded as a classic of its type. A clockwork motor enables the rider to mount, ride and jump off the machine whilst the engine ticks over. Beautifully made and of obvious quality; £700 boxed

marques such as Harley Davidson. The Chinese have recently begun making tinplate clockwork-operated motorcycle toys. They do not compare in quality to the earlier German or Japanese toys but they are easily available and are cheap.

METAL

Although seldom seen for sale, full-size and half-size replicas of real motorcycles have been made by various specialist manufacturers, not as toys but as fairground carousel items. These rare items are always popular with toy motorcycle collectors but are more often than not acquired on the open market by interior designers and command high prices.

DIECAST

One of the earlier examples of a motorcycle in diecast is the series of cyclists made by Meccano in their Dinky (q.v.) range of toys. They were small in size (under 2 inches in length) and comprised civilian riders, army despatch riders, AA and RAC patrolmen. They were first made in the late 1930s and all pre-war types were issued with white rubber tyres. Although they are now over 50 years old they often turn up at jumble sales and are not expensive.

Three Motorcycles from Lesney. These appeal to motorcyclists as well as Matchbox enthusiasts and have always commanded a premium over cars. The scooter is worth £25, the others £40 each boxed

Lesney Products introduced two motorcycles without riders into the 'Matchbox' Series range in the 1960s. It is still possible to find mint and boxed examples of the No. 4 Triumph T110 issued in July 1960 in a metallic blue livery, the No. 66 Harley Davidson issued in a metallic copper finish in October 1962 and the No. 38 Honda Motorcycle and Trailer issued in metallic blue in September 1969. Matchless Toys Ltd (q.v.) also issued a Sunbeam Motorcycle in 1962 in the Models of Yesteryear range. Other British diecast toy manufacturers such as Benbros (q.v.) and Morestone produced diecast motorcycles, with the most

This 1930s Motorcycle and Sidecar exudes quality and charm and was made by Tipp & Co.; £400 unboxed

This Fire Department Motorcyclist is from the 1950s; c £90 unboxed. Also illustrated is a Scooter and Rider, produced by Einfelt c 1954. Though clearly not of the quality of other German toys, it compensates for this by the colourful and charming use of lithographic decoration. All motorcycles are of necessity fragile and so a survivor in good condition will always be collectable; c £90

common theme being breakdown services such as the AA and the RAC. A good selection of expensive diecast motorcycles was made by the Danish firm of Tekno during the 1960s. These are seldom seen for sale except in specialist toy shops. During the 1970s Britains Ltd (q.v.) produced a good range of motorcycle toys, in both diecast and plastic.

PLASTIC

One of the best examples known of plastic motorcycles is undoubtedly the Tri-ang-Minic Mota-Scoot (see Minic) which operated on a 'push and go' mechanism. It was a well-made representation of a young 'mod' with scarf flying behind on his 1950s-style Vespa. Although some collectors may not like the feel of plastic toys, they would be hard pressed to find much wrong with this toy. It is much sought after by collectors and has been offered with a price tag of £85. *See also: Battery Toys; Novelty Toys.*

Manufacturers
Alps (q.v.), Arnold (q.v.), Einfelt (q.v.), Lesney (q.v.), Tipp and Co (q.v.).

· NOVELTY ·
· TOYS ·

Such toys are ones that appeal to the
collector, not only because they are
attractive and pleasantly represent a real
human or animal figure or object, but
also because a main feature of such
items is an amusing mechanism which
can often overshadow any intended
realism. The toy can be classified as a
novelty toy if it is amusing, clever and
brings a smile to the child or collector.
The most common mechanism used
was a clockwork motor, and the
movements could vary in sophistication
from an arm being lifted to a toy
monkey doing handstands! Collectable
novelty toys up to the 1950s were made
from tin. This medium was replaced by
plastic and celluloid in the late 1950s
and early 1960s when the Japanese toy
manufacturers began to make copies of
earlier tinplate novelty toys.

TINPLATE

The majority of novelty tinplate
clockwork-operated toys were originally
made in Germany. Most of the famous
toy manufacturers turned their attention
to this ever-popular range of toy, the
most prolific being Lehmann (q.v.).
Tom the Climbing Monkey dressed in
tail-coat and sporting a red fez could

Gustav the Climbing Miller
is a famous toy justifiably
so for the ingenious
method of its operation.
The Miller climbs the
ladder and deposits a sack
of flour at the top of the
mill. Produced in large
quantities in the 1920s by
Lehmann; £150

The Balky Mule emulates
the antics of a circus act,
once a form of popular
entertainment but now
quickly disappearing.
Eminently collectable;
£175 boxed

Dancing Couple—this charming toy executes a waltz when wound and was made by Guntermann but distributed by Moko in 1906. Even in this distressed condition it is worth £350

Sparking 'Doughboy' Tank—a familiar toy and produced in great quantities but today hard to find in complete and working condition. The example shown here dates from 1935 but there are other detail variations; £150 boxed

climb up a rope, while Gustav the Miller could shin up a pole carrying a sack of flour on his head. This company made hundreds of different novelty toys, the majority of which were boxed. The original box often provides the maker's name and instructions on how to operate the toy.

Technofix (the trademark of G. Einfelt (q.v.)) made a series of clockwork tinplate toys using tracked vehicles. The toys were popular not only for their play value but also for their attractive, vivid colours. Some of their toys used alpine scenery and would have cable cars travelling over a valley; tinplate clockwork cars featured driving down the mountain road – and all this on one toy! In recent years, tinplate manufacturers in the Eastern Bloc have made toys very similar in concept to Technofix toys, and although easy to find today may provide some collectable interest in the future.

Another German toy company, Schuco, also made novelty toys. In particular, their range of musicians are most sought after. These figures are just under 5 inches in height and include a drummer and a violinist. Other figures were also made, the most famous of which was the clown who could juggle balls in the air. The figures were dressed in a cloth fabric and were made

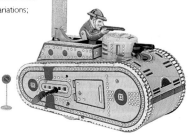

This Carousel dates from 1910 which may be hard to believe judging by the freshness of its airbrush applied finish. This toy features a beautifully precise and well engineered clockwork movement, fitted with a free wheel device which enables the carousel to continue some time after the motor has unwound. For a rare toy such as this to survive unmarked is most unusual; £500 unboxed

both before and after World War II.

Arnold (q.v.), also a Germany company, made a great range of novelty toys, the most famous being a motorcyclist known as Mac. The cyclist and the motorcycle were both realistic and would satisfy the needs of any collector interested in motorbikes. However, the ingenuity of the toy is only apparent when the clockwork motor is wound up . . . after travelling in a circle the rider would dismount, stand by the bike, move his leg back over the saddle, sit down and drive off. The toy had several settings which could be pre-set by the child to determine what movements he wished his rider to do.

In many ways the archetypal toy for young children, novelty toys such as these concentrated on movement and action to catch the young eye. These are now becoming collectable under the Minic brand name. The Jabberwak is worth £45 and the Drummer Clown by Schuco c 1950 about £60

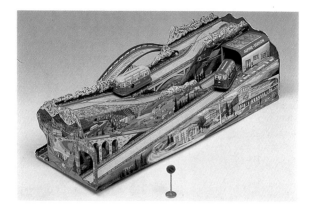

Alpine Express. This attractive toy by Einfalt is both ingenious and colourful. These were produced up to the 1950s; £150 boxed

PLASTIC

After World War II, many of the pre-war well-known German toy manufacturers did not start up in business again. With the exception of manufacturers such as Schuco, Einfelt and Arnold, the market was wide open for the Japanese. In most cases they turned away from the more expensive tin toys and instead launched a vast array of novelty toys made from cheaper materials such as plastic. They retained the clockwork mechanisms and in many cases copied earlier German novelty toys. As they gained in confidence, they began to develop their own ideas and had by the late 1950s established themselves as equally good toy makers. Although many collectors do not like plastic, Japanese novelty toys of this era are becoming quite valuable. As with battery toys, the Japanese changed direction in the 1960s by developing computer orientated toys with the effect that they no longer manufactured the most traditional toy, i.e. clockwork-driven toys.

The Chinese then carried on and they in turn began making copies of the Japanese novelty toys. Although they have now begun making original toys, they can still be found for sale at low prices in most toy and hobby shops. It is unlikely that they will ever become truly collectable. The British firm Lies Bros. (q.v.) issued an extensive range of plastic novelty toys during the 1950s under the Tri-ang Minic brand name. Minic (q.v.), who had for many years made brightly coloured tinplate clockwork vehicles, had realised that the medium of plastic was the new material for the 1950s and 1960s. Few British toy manufacturers in the post-war era were making novelty toys and so Minic quickly saw their opportunity. One of the most common Minic plastic novelty toys is the crocodile toy called Jabberwock. They also made a pecking bird, a walking sailor and a spider. They are not expensive to buy and are growing quickly in popularity with collectors of novelty toys, who are now finding it difficult to buy tinplate toys at reasonable prices.

In considering a collection of novelty toys it would pay to specialise in an area of interest either by the type of toy or the manufacturer. This need not be restricting as the comprehensive range covered by Tri-ang Minic exceeds 100 items, for example. The normal considerations of display space should never be overlooked. *See also: Figures; Motorcycles; Plastic Toys.*

Manufacturers
Arnold (q.v.), Einfelt (q.v.), Lehmann (q.v.), Schuco, Tri-ang Minic.

This Japanese Circus Car is one of the last generation of tinplate toys from the early 1960s. The value of toys such as these can only appreciate as time passes; worth £50

· PEDAL · CARS ·

Within a few years of the automobile
becoming a common sight, children's
pedal-powered replicas were being
produced. In some cases they were
made by the car manufacturer such as
Citroën and Bugatti and in other cases
by toy manufacturers, the biggest being
Lines Bros. (q.v.) (Tri-ang). By the
early 1920s sophisticated pedal cars
were on the market – although only the
rich could afford them. Like the real car
they were available with oil lamps,
petrol cans, working horns, lights,
pneumatic tyres, leather seats and
wooden steering wheels. These early
examples featured a chain link
mechanism similar to a bicycle.
Materials used were predominantly
wood or sheet metal. Shortly after
World War I the manufacturers
developed an easier means of propelling
the car: a crank back axle with pedal-
activated connecting rods. Wood was
replaced entirely by sheet metal.

Production of pedal cars continued
after World War II but the expense of
producing magnificent small-scale
replicas of such marques as Rolls-Royce
and Bugatti proved to be uneconomical.

Pedal cars vary in quality
from the cheap and
cheerful Tri-ang 'Royal
Prince' shown here to
hand made Rolls Royce
and Bugatti replicas.
Collectors should ensure
that they have the space
to store and display them;
£75

The designers tended to make smaller-sized cars with fewer accessories. The most famous post-war pedal car is possily the Austin cars made during the 1950s. Two types were made: the saloon and the A40 racer. Both cars were made from sheet metal remnants from the Austin factory which were sent down to south Wales where disabled miners turned the metal into pedal cars. They were often used by Austin car dealers in sales promotions. In all, some 32,000 of the J40 were made and each one carries a serial number on the bottom lid of the boot.

As with vintage collectors' cars, it is rare to find a pedal car in absolutely mint condition. A pedal car in a rusty and distressed condition but with the potential to be restored will still be of value to a pedal car enthusiast. Missing parts such as steering wheels or hub caps can be a problem but these can often be found for sale at general auto jumbles. Much of the pleasure in pedal cars can be the challenge of restoration, but often the car's restored value does not reflect the work that went into it.

Other types of vehicles have been used as pedal cars, such as aeroplanes, trains and boats.

During the 1970s and up to the present day, toy manufacturers have continued to make pedal cars, not in metal but in plastic. Similar in size to metal pedal cars they may well become collectors' items in the future but storage and display space may be the overriding disadvantage for the average collector. A J40 pedal car is nearly 5 feet long and 3 feet wide and needs two people to lift it.

Manufacturers
ELR (East London Rubber Co.), Lines Bros. (q.v.).

· PENNY · TOYS ·

A range of unsophisticated tinplate toys made from the early 1900s up to just after World War I measuring no more than 3.5 inches high and 3–4 inches in length and originally costing up to a few pennies each. The vast majority of penny toys were made in Germany and were imported in bulk into Britain by wholesalers who in turn would have supplied market traders or street vendors. The modern-day equivalent would be the trader selling inflated balloons from a hastily created stall in the middle of a shopping precinct.

The majority of penny toys were highly coloured. Some had simple movements such as wheels on cars or rockers under a horse, and in some cases a flywheel drive to enable the toy to do something a little more interesting such as gnomes beating the anvil with their hammers or cutting a log with their saws. Due to their size and original popularity many penny toys have not survived. They can be found but are often broken or have parts missing.

These penny toys from 1910 were originally sold for 1 penny each on street corners. The lithography on these beautiful objects would be difficult to produce in this day and age; £100 each

Only a few will form an attractive grouping, and they are expensive.

Manufacturers
Kellermann (q.v.).

· PLASTIC · KITS ·

These are becoming collectable, especially kits from the 1950s. Airfix (q.v.) is possibly the most well-known manufacturer, closely followed by Revell, AMT and Matchbox (q.v.). The rule of thumb for desirability is that boxed kits fetch much greater prices than assembled kits.

Check copyright information on boxes where possible to date a kit, as often the manufacturer will relaunch a good seller, an example being the Matchbox Corvette kit which was originally made in the early 1970s and reissued in 1985.

Airfix were to dominate the market in the late 1950s and early 1960s with their very inexpensive and large range of cars, ships, aeroplanes and model figures. Some specific models were (for reasons unknown) to become extremely rare; an example of this is a Westland

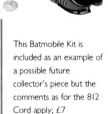

This Batmobile Kit is included as an example of a possible future collector's piece but the comments as for the 812 Cord apply; £7

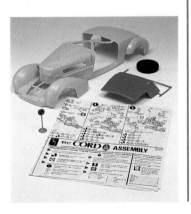

A superb model of an 812 Cord produced by AMT in the 1970s. These cannot really be classed as a sound investment because the huge tooling costs required to produce a kit means that the tools would not have been destroyed and could be used to introduce the kit; £20.

Helicopter in BEA livery. Athough as previously stated the unmade kit is more valuable, it is very much up to the individual whether or not he finds the kit more satisfying as a completed model than as a number of parts.

Manufacturers
Airfix (q.v.), AMT, Ertl (q.v.), Monogram, Pyro, Revell.

· PLASTIC · · TOYS ·

As a material used in toy manufacturing plastic is now one of the most important. However, for collectors it has never been regarded with much affection. Plastic came into prominence during the late 1950s and was used by the manufacturers as part of a cost-reducing exercise and as a way to make more complex shapes and colours. An acceptable compromise is when a toy has been made, for example, out of diecast or tin and extra detail has been included in plastic. There are, of course, exceptions, usually where a toy with a big collecting potential has been made only in plastic and never, for example, in diecast or tinplate. Examples include a toy of Sting-ray made entirely out of plastic and operated by batteries (from

Early TV related toys are a good and unusual subject to collect. This large model of the Sting Ray is worth £75 boxed

the famous television programme from the early 1960s) or the all-plastic Dalek made in 1964 under the Codeg brand

$\mathcal{P}$

This interesting model of James Bond's Aston Martin is worth £200 boxed. The superb scale model of an Austin Healey 100/6 was made in 1960. Not successful then but the growth of the classic car market has led to an appreciation of this detailed model. Inherently fragile, these are not easy to find complete; £150 boxed

name to represent the machines in the *Dr Who* television programme.

Plastic toys from the 1950s and 1960s could be one of the future collectables, especially the super range of large-scale plastic electric model cars made by Tri-ang Minic (see Minic) in the very early 1960s. They were made entirely from plastic and were operated by two batteries concealed under the body. The range included a Triumph Herald, Morris Mini Minor, Ford Zephyr and Caravan and sports cars such as the Austin Healey 100/6. They were all 1/20 scale and are collected not only by Tri-ang Minic collectors but enthusiasts of the real car such as the MGA or the Healey. Tri-ang Minic also produced a range of plastic novelty toys in the 1950s which included a clockwork mouse and a ladybird. These are inexpensive to buy and make for an interesting collection. Check for cracks as old plastic can become brittle. *See also: Character Toys, Novelty Toys, Minic.*

Manufacturers
Cowan de Groot (q.v.), Tri-ang Minic.

· ROBOTS ·

Battery-operated robots from the 1950s and 1960s have become the most popular of all battery-operated toys. Today they are collected not only by robot enthusiasts but also battery toy and science fiction collectors.

Robots are described as being man-made machines capable of doing human deeds and the term 'robot' is derived from the Czechoslovakian word 'robota' which means 'forced labour'! Robot toys are often mistaken for astronaut toys which are human beings inside space suits!

It must be remembered that when robot toys were introduced to children the robot was a mysterious concept that was not an everyday occurrence. The toys from the 1950s were often more

Even plastic robots such as this (left) from the early 1970s are collectable today. The functions of robots in plastic often exceed those of the tinplate type; £35. The tinplate version is a well-known example; £75 unboxed

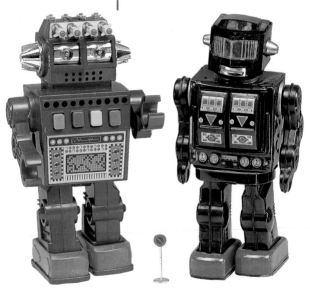

sophisticated and advanced than the actual robots being developed by the scientists. The inclusion of robots into contemporary films (*War of the Worlds* or *The Day The Earth Stood Still*) and television programmes helped to advance the sophistication of the robot. Now that scientists have caught up with the movie makers, present-day robot toys do not have the same charm or inherent nostalgia.

Materials used to make robot toys include tin, plastic, rubber and cloth. One of the most famous robot toys is 'Robbie the Robot', based on the robot in the movie *The Forbidden Planet*. He could walk and at the same time pistons in his head moved up and down while the antennae in his ears rotated.

Today robot toys are still being made in countries such as Macau or Hong Kong with the biggest market for modern-day robots being the USA. When beginning a collection remember the larger the better, and the more movements the better. Robot toys based on successful films or television programmes are more sought after than ones featured in programmes that were short-lived. *See also: Space Toys, Battery Toys.*

Manufacturers
Alps (q.v.), Bandai (q.v.), Daiya, Ichida, Linemar (q.v.), Nomura, Yoshiya (all Japanese) and Cragstan – an importer of toys.

· SOLDIERS ·

Most boys have played with toy soldiers. By the middle of the 18th century soldier figures were being made primarily to teach the sons of the aristocracy how famous battles had been won or lost and to learn modern warfare techniques. These early figures were made from tin and were flat in appearance, not a full, rounded representation of the human form. However, the famous royal families of Europe often commissioned individuals to make model armies using silver and pewter. By the middle of the 19th century, lead had become the most popular medium. The figures remained solid, flat and highly coloured. Famous makers include Hilbert and Stahl, Gottschak, Wehrli, Mignot, Lucotte and Heyde. Toy soldiers made by these manufacturers never appear on the general antiques market.

LEAD

In 1893 W. Britains of England invented a technique to replace the then

Genuine lead soldiers such as these examples by Britains from the 1940s cannot be mistaken for modern copies and usually have a patina of age. These Welsh Fusiliers and World War I infantry are worth £10 each

popular semi-flat figures. His technique
allowed the figure to be hollow and
realistically proportioned. Lighter and
cheaper than their foreign counterparts,
Britains' soldiers became a presence in
children's bedrooms for about 70 years.
His firm paid great attention to detail
and ensured that correct uniforms,
weapons and colours were used. Within
a short time his toy soldiers were being
bought by adults, not just for their
children but for themselves. There was
no shortage of play value because many
of the soldiers were made with moving
arms: soldiers could then point their
rifles and bayonets and native troops
could wave their spears! With the
introduction of khaki in 1898 during the
South African Campaign, children
rejected the earlier more colourful
uniforms and revamped their own
troops. Britains followed suit and began
producing soldiers in khaki. Each set
(there were usually eight figures to a
set) came packaged in a dark red box,
the lid bearing a paper label identifying
the contents.

Britains make
commemorative sets today
in metal, usually limited to
5,000 sets. These
attractive Parachute
Regiment Colours Party
retail at £35. Their
investment appeal is as yet
an unknown quantity

Elastolin figures are fragile and therefore rare. They are a subject for specialised collecting but may well turn up anonymously at car boot fairs; £28 each

Today there is a vast following for Britains lead soldiers, especially in the UK and the USA (as many as 100 million figures were exported to the USA during the 1920s and 1930s). After World War II production was slow in starting and it was during the early 1950s that plastic was identified as being the new medium to use. Lead was no longer in fashion and plastic was cheaper. Although of limited appeal, the plastic figures of the 1950s and 1960s are steadily becoming more valuable. Britains returned to diecast and launched a range of toy soldiers to complement their plastic range in 1973. To cater for present-day collectors who like the idea of a limited edition set, Britains have introduced in the last few years good quality metal figures based on sets they have made in past years. Some of these have been limited to only 5000 sets and could well prove to be an investment for the future.

Britains had to contend with rival toy companies who soon learned to manufacture using the hollow-cast process. In fact, John Hill Co was

founded by an ex-Britains employee.
Although in many cases toy soldiers
made by John Hill Co were as good in
detail as Britains', the collectors' market
puts a higher premium on Britains' toy
soldiers. This can also be said for the
other English companies that rivalled
Britains for business, such as Taylor &
Barratt, W. T. Courtenay, Timpo (q.v.),
Charbens (q.v.) and Crescent Toys
(q.v.).

ELASTOLIN

Not all toy soldiers were made from tin,
pewter, lead, diecast or plastic. A
compound material known as Elastolin
was successfully used by several
German toy soldier manufacturers
during the 1920s and 1930s. The
compound was made from a mixture of
sawdust, resin and glue which was
moulded around a wire structure. They
were, unfortunately, fragile and more
often than not are found with missing
feet, hands or heads. The two most
famous manufacturers who used
Elastolin were Hausser (q.v.) and
Lineol. Hausser made two different-
sized figures: 40 mm and 54 mm, and
varied their subject matter from English
Grenadier Guards to the German army
of pre-war and World War II. Both
these manufacturers made figures of
Hitler which command high prices
when they turn up at auctions or for sale
in specialist shops.

Damaged toy soldiers made from
Elastolin can be successfully repaired.
This may, however, adversely affect the
value of the figure.

PLASTIC

Possibly the most famous British plastic
toy soldier manufacturer was Herald
Miniatures, who in 1953 released
several plastic figures some of which
were soldiers: Highland soldiers,

Herald were a significant manufacturer of both metal and plastic figures in the 1960s and 1970s. Their plastic figures are becoming more collectable and these 1970s specimens are worth £4 each

infantry soldiers and Scots Guards soldiers. Plastic figures became established quickly – parents liked them because they were considerably cheaper than lead/metal figures to buy and nearly impossible to break, and children liked them because they were more realistic.

Historical themes were later introduced. In 1959 Herald, now part of Britains, released soldiers from the English Civil War. There was also a range of American Civil War soldiers. However, the most famous range, introduced in 1961, was the 'Eyes Right': the figures had movable heads and detachable arms and bodies. Boxed sets of the US Marine Band, Scots Guards and Royal Marine Corps to name just a few are much sought after. Herald Miniatures had by now become totally integrated with Britains, and as such the 'Eyes Right' range was entirely marketed as a Britains product. In the early 1970s a new range of military figures under the brand name of Deetail was launched – soldiers from World War II dominated this range and include German soldiers and British Paratroopers. These plastic figures were secured to a metal baseplate.

Toy soldiers have proved a steady investment. Full sets, preferably boxed, are most desirable. Check that each figure is part of the set and that where relevant they are identical. Try to avoid broken figures unless the missing parts are available for restoration. *See also: Animal Figures.*

Manufacturers
Britains (q.v.), Crescent (q.v.), Hausser (q.v.), Lineol, Timpo (q.v.).

Britains modelled every type of regiment known. This group of Royal Marines from the 1930s is worth £10 each unboxed

· SPACE · TOYS ·

This is a category of toy that is becoming more and more popular. Space toys such as rockets and astronauts that are characteristic of the real race for space which began in the early 1960s overlap easily with character/TV-related fictitious space-related toys as portrayed in programmes such as *Fire Ball XL5*, *Thunderbirds* and *Space 1999*.

Examples of astronaut (cosmonaut) toys are quite rare, especially ones made out of tin and battery operated.

Space Patrol Car illustrates the fascination the concept of space held for the toy manufacturer and the public alike. This well preserved example from the late 1950s is worth £90 unboxed

Astronaut toys made during the 1950s are of greatest interest to collectors because the toys were developed from what the designers considered astronauts would look like or what they had been told they would look like from books or films. The example shown was made during the 1950s. Powered by battery, he walks forward, stops, lifts his gun with both hands and shoots – all with sound effects and flashing lights. This toy was made by Daiya of Japan and distributed throughout the world by the Cragstan organisation. This particular example is, unfortunately, missing his antenna.

Easier to obtain are space-related toys made in diecast and produced in the main by Dinky Toys (q.v.). A good representation of the US Shuttle was produced in the late 1970s. Fictitious toys such as the USS Enterprise from the *Star Trek* television series, International Rescue vehicles from the *Thunderbirds* series and Supercar (made by Budgie) once again based on the 1960s television series, are all very much sought after.

Space-related toy watches have also

Illustrated here is a rare Astronaut in blue finish, dating from the late 1950s. Although the antenna is missing, it is nevertheless worth £150 unboxed

These two diecast toys, although initially ignored, have now become very sought after by Dinky toy and space toy collectors. The Shuttle Craft dates back to 1978; £50 boxed. The Thunderbird 2 is from 1968; £100

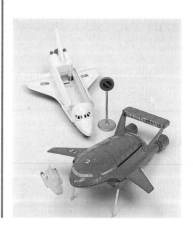

Although flying saucers were normally the preserve of mysterious aliens, this example has changed sides and is flying on behalf of NASA! It is very rare to find an example in this condition and it is worth £150 boxed

been popular with collectors. One example is a toy pocket watch with Dan Dare featured on the watchface. Such an item would be highly regarded by a collector of space-related toys.

The popularity of the film or television programme often has a bearing on the popularity of the toy. It is important that all parts to the toy are complete, e.g. Thunderbird 5 came as part of the Thunderbird 2 (made by Dinky). The original box adds to the value. *See also: Character toys; Robots.*

Manufacturers
Alps Linemar, Bandai (q.v.), Budgie, Bullmark, Dinky (q.v.), Ichida, Nomura.

Dan Dare toys, once cheap and plentiful, are now very scarce. This watch, not attributed to a manufacturer nor particularly attractive, dates from the 1950s; £60

This unlikely looking Rocket Fighter from 1960 emits sparks and an engine rattle when driven; £40

· SPOT-ON ·

This short-lived range of diecast model road-going vehicles was introduced by Tri-ang (see Minic) (the Lines Bros. Group (q.v.)) in 1959. The manufacturing plant on the Castlereagh Road in Belfast, Northern Ireland, was closed in 1967 through indifferent sales' success. Limited production was continued in New Zealand for four years before final cessation of production in 1970. They are considered by many diecast collectors to be one of the finest ranges of models. Spot-On models were always made to the constant scale of 1/43 (slightly larger than the rival Dinky (q.v.) toys they were competing with) and were always painted in the colour schemes of the actual vehicles, unlike for example Corgi (q.v.) or Lesney (q.v.) who would

This selection of Spot-On vehicles has been professionally restored to the highest standard; worth £20 each

paint them in colours that they knew would appeal to children rather than model car enthusiasts.

The Spot-On range, which includes saloons, sports cars, buses and heavy goods lorries, became very collectable in the mid-1980s. Prices escalated from the usual price of £40 for a saloon car up to £80–£100 within a year. Many speculator collectors entered the 'hobby' and began buying every single Spot-On model they could. There appeared to be a great demand for Spot-On models and it also appeared that there were hundreds of Spot-On collectors in Britain alone. In fact, this was not the case, and with hindsight it now appears that one or two dealers hyped up the market for Spot-On models. Rumours abounded at toy fairs about just how desirable and collectable Spot-On models were, but many collectors who quickly built up a collection found to their dismay that a Spot-On model was not such a good buy as many dealers had long since moved out of Spot-On trading and suddenly there was little interest left in the range.

On the positive side, however, Spot-On were beautifully made diecast models and are eagerly collected by 'marque' enthusiasts such as Rolls-Royce, Bentley, Sunbeam Alpines or Bristols. Prices have levelled off recently and mint boxed examples of standard range models can usually be purchased for £50–£60.

Mint boxed examples of Spot-On models are virtually impossible to find, but scratched examples do turn up regularly. These are ideal subjects for restoration, as the photograph shows, and can form the basis of an inexpensive collection. *See also: Cars; Lines Bros.*
Trademark
Spot-On.

· TEDDY · BEARS ·

Although soft toy manufacturers had made toy bears by the turn of the century, it was only when a cartoon appeared in an American newspaper in 1902 showing President Theodore Roosevelt refusing to shoot a bear cub that a new name for toy bears came into being: Teddy's bear or, as it was soon to become, Teddy Bear.

This form of toy has always been popular with children mainly because they are soft and comforting. As often as not teddy bears seen for sale will usually show signs of wear and tear – a chewed ear or a missing arm that has been pulled off in a tug-of-war! Constant use over the years can also lead to alopecia and patches of hair so worn away that all that is left is the original fabric underneath the fur.

The more collectable teddy bears are those that have jointed arms and legs as opposed to bears that are stitched into place. Many bears were fitted with growler boxes, which are usually to be found stitched inside the tummy. The

News-media publicity has misguided the public as to the real values of teddy bears. This 1940s Teddy Bear is unusual being open mouthed and is worth £200. The much smaller teddy, also from the 1940s, is worth £50

Steiff teddies of any size command a premium and this example from the 1930s is worth £100. It is more valuable than the medium sized English version; £75

older bears were filled with wood, wool and sawdust which during the 1930s became Kapok and later foam padding. Older bears also had leather pads on the paws and feet. This was later substituted by Leatherette and even later plastic or felt. Early bears had black metal shoe buttons for eyes and these later changed to glass eyes.

The teddy bear has changed gradually in appearance since its inception in the early 1900s. Instead of a rather pronounced pointed snout, contemporary bears have much more rounded noses. Early bears also featured humped backs. The fabric used to simulate the fur has also changed from the early mohair plush fabric to modern-day nylon imitation fur.

The most famous teddy bear manufacturer is without doubt the German company of Steiff (q.v.), who made it easy to identify their bears by clipping a button on one of the bear's ears. Although mint (unused) teddy bears made by Steiff can fetch prices in the tens of thousands of pounds, they can still be found for sale in non-specialist toy shops or local fairs. The

Steiff company have continued to produce teddy bears and today cater for teddy bear collectors by reissuing classic teddy bears that they made in previous decades. Although they are relatively expensive they could well be collectable toys of the future. They are bought by collectors but are equally attractive to parents or grandparents looking for a nostalgic classic toy for their children.

Although the Steiff bear is the most desirable, English companies such as Merrythought are also sought after. Today several teddy bear companies have established themselves in the market of making collectable/traditional teddy bears. One of the better-known ones is the Yorkshire firm Gabrielle, who also have the licence to make Paddington Bear.

Often the larger bears are more desirable than smaller bears. Condition of fur and movement of joints, leather pads and straw filling are all factors that influence the value. Shape and size of nose can indicate the age of the bear. A maker's identification mark or label is quite important.

Manufacturers
Chad Valley (q.v.), Merrythought, Steiff (q.v.), Swan.

· TELEVISION ·
· TOYS ·
See Character Toys

· TRAINS ·
HORNBY

Undoubtedly the most famous British toy train manufacturer was Meccano Ltd (q.v.). Frank Hornby, who founded Meccano Ltd in 1901, turned his attention to developing a railway system

Two extremely sought after engines by Hornby from the pre-war era of O Gauge. These have appreciated rapidly over the years and a Royal Scot is worth £400 boxed, whilst the Lord Nelson is worth £300

that was comparable to the quality of the German toy train manufacturers. He built up a good business relationship with the Marklin company who made clockwork motors for the early Meccano construction toys. He was convinced that the British could make equally good trains. During the period of World War I he researched and developed his first train by using many of the parts found in a standard Meccano set and as a result this train was bolted together. This technique was then improved so that the construction was hardly noticeable. Hornby also used the less expensive process of tabbing over the component pieces of tin and in general terms this process was restricted to their cheaper ranges. Most of the German firms had used large gauges, i.e. the size of the gauge (scale) states the distance between the inner edges of the track. Hornby felt that the large gauges were far too big for an average-sized house and so made his trains to 'O' Gauge which equates to a track distance of 1.25 inches. He was later to reduce the gauge to 'OO' (.625 inches).

Hornby trains were originally fitted with robust clockwork motors. In 1925 Hornby introduced his first electric train – a Metropolitan locomotive and two coaches. This was of great interest to enthusiasts who were frustrated with clockwork trains that needed to be continually wound up. However, not everybody had electricity in the early 1920s and the Hornby system was somewhat basic. The electricity supply had to be capped by additional regulators and resistors. These electric trains ran on a three-rail track – the centre rail was live and made contact with the pick-up on the underside of the locomotive. Clockwork trains also used the same standard three-rail track.

Post 1945 Hornby trains became smaller and simpler, the 1950s type 501 with tender is worth £135 boxed. Obviously, far fewer trains were produced than rolling stock. This example of rolling stock is worth £20 boxed

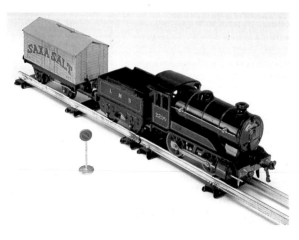

During the late 1920s and 1930s Hornby introduced a vast range of locomotives, tank engines, tenders, pullman coaches, brake vans and wagons all sporting literally hundreds of different liveries. Many of the trains were made with or without electric motors, examples being the magnificent Royal Scot and the Lord Nelson. Although both are equally valuable, the electrified versions have more appeal and are eagerly sought after by collectors today who 'run' their trains, as opposed to those who display them only.

The most impressive 'O' Gauge Hornby train is probably the L.M.S. (London Midland and Scottish Railway) 4–6–2 (these numbers refer to the wheel pattern) Princess Elizabeth, which was issued in 1938. A relatively

All Hornby Dublo metal cast locomotives are now valuable. This Nigel Greasley is worth £70 boxed and the breakdown crane set £25 boxed

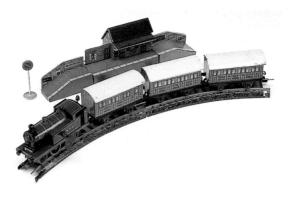

t

This 1920s Bing 'Table' Railway was one of the first OO Gauge sets and may have been the inspiration for Hornby Dublo; £100 boxed

small number of these beautiful 20-volt trains were made with an original selling price of five guineas. Special 3-foot-radius steel tracks had to be made as the standard track curve would never have held the train. Most Princess Elizabeth trains suffered wheel metal fatigue but replacement wheels can be obtained through vintage toy train outlets and do not have an adverse effect on the value of the train. Although mint and boxed examples of the train command prices in excess of £2000, such a train that has the potential to be professionally restored could be worth at least £750. The S.R. (Southern Railway) 4-4-0 Eton made at the same time is also one of the most valuable Hornby trains of this era – prices for a good mint boxed example range from £500 to £700.

At the lower end of the price scale are the Hornby 'O' Gauge tank trains which are, of course, less impressive than the larger locomotives and which come in two basic sizes – the large No. 2 Specials (4-4-2) and No. 1 Specials (0-4-0) and the smaller No. 1 and M3 type. A much cheaper range of tabbed-over trains, known as the 'M' series, was first released in the 1930s. This particular range, although quite attractive, does

not have real appeal to train collectors –
the value of a mint boxed example
being in the £30 to £40 range.

As a general dating guide, all pre-war
Hornby trains were marked Hornby
Series. Post-war items were marked
Hornby Trains. After the war,
production of the 'O' Gauge range
continued although as discussed below
the 'OO' Gauge series was seen as
being the way forward. More emphasis
was put on tank trains, well-known
examples being the 501 trains. Many of
the post-war items were sold as sets, i.e.
a train, tender, carriages and track.
Although single electric trains were
made, these were mostly aimed at the
export market. Rolling stock was,
however, made in large quantities.
Some of the pre-war liveries were
reissued but new designs such as the
Saxa Salt Wagon were also introduced.
As with the pre-war range, Hornby
issued a large range of tinplate/metal
stations, signals, buffers etc. These too
are eagerly sought after. The average
value for post-war rolling stock is in the
region of £20 for a mint boxed item
compared to £40 to £50 for its pre-war
equivalent. Hornby ceased production
of its 'O' Gauge range in the early 1960s.

In 1938, two years after the death of
Sir Frank Hornby, the company
introduced a range of trains and rolling
stock called Hornby Dublo (OO
Gauge). Both clockwork-operated and
electric trains were introduced, the first
train being the L.N.E.R.(London and
North Eastern Railways) 4–6–2 Sir
Nigel Gresley in blue. This train was
also made after the war. It was,
however, modified so that the wheels
were exposed whereas pre-war
examples were closed in. Initially all
early Hornby Dublo trains were made
in diecast and all associated rolling stock

Rarer than Hornby and always beautifully made, this carriage by Bing is to Gauge 0 scale from the 1930s; £130

was made from tin and diecast. Originally the track was three-rail but was later changed to two-rail. In 1958 Meccano introduced a range of miniature OO gauge vehicles known as Dinky Dublo models. These were bought by railway enthusiasts to add realism to their layouts. These models were marked as Dinky Dublo and examples include Bedford articulated flat trucks, a taxi and even a tractor. Mint boxed examples are reasonably easy to find and are priced between £25 and £45. The use of plastic became more common from the early 1960s and much of the rolling stock was converted from tin to plastic.

Early Dublo trains and rolling stock were packaged in blue and white boxes. These are more desirable than the red boxes introduced in the late 1950s. Although Dublo was made by Tri-ang after Lines Bros. bought out Meccano in 1964, they do not have the same collectability as Hornby Dublo. Changes to the range included the moving away from diecast trains to plastic ones. These, of course, are relatively popular with today's OO gauge enthusiasts because it is relatively inexpensive to buy a Tri-ang locomotive – mint and boxed about £15. After the many changes of the Lines Bros. fortune, the Hornby range of trains and rolling stock is being made today by the firm of

Hornby Hobbies which is based in Kent. *See also: Dinky (q.v.)*, *Lines Bros. (q.v.)*, *Meccano (q.v.)*, *Tri-ang.*

GERMAN MANUFACTURERS

Famous toy makers, including Carette (q.v.), Marklin and Bing (q.v.), pioneered the development of tinplate/metal trains during the late 19th and early 20th centuries. The majority of these firms had been established in Nuremberg, the clock-making region of Germany, and it was a relatively simple matter to modify their mechanisms to fit all sorts of trains and toys. Steam-powered trains were also made. During this period the Germans produced their trains in Gauge 3, 2 and 1. These were considerably larger in size than Gauge O (described above) and most impressive, their size enabling the designers to include the smallest details. However, they were expensive to produce and they could only be afforded by the wealthiest families. By the outbreak of World War I most of the German firms had reduced their products down to Gauge O. Examples of these early German toy trains are very rare and command extremely high prices. In general terms they are bought by collectors who wish to have them on display rather than running them. After the war, Bing introduced their Miniature Table Railway in 1922 in OO Gauge. These have become very collectable in recent years.

During the early part of the 20th century Bing began to export their range to W. J. Bassett-Lowke who was based in Northampton, who acted initially as a distributor, but by the 1920s he was successfully producing his own range of trains. These were intended to be models rather than toys and were always marketed as being scale models. As models, they fall outside the scope of this publication.

In the 1930s the German firm Trix (q.v.) successfully introduced their range of electric-powered OO Gauge railways. The firm had a tie-in with Bassett-Lowke (q.v.) and in 1935 moved from Germany to Northampton. Early tinplate Trix is sought after by collectors. The Bing company was taken over by the Bub (q.v.) firm in 1933 and Bub continued to make OO Gauge railways right up to 1967. Although their later product was made mostly from plastic, they were highly regarded by toy train collectors.

WALLWORKS

Cast-iron non-motorised trains made by the Wallworks Company of Manchester are quite common. A small range of these toy trains were made in the 1890s as a means of using up surplus material. They are extremely heavy and with time are usually found suffering the effects of rust. There is, however, a pleasing appeal from these toy trains and they do not look out of place beside tinplate trains. *See also: Bassett-Lowke; Bing; Bub; Carette.*

This cast iron train by Wallworks is virtually indestructible. It dates back to 1890 but its material ensured its survival; £200

manufacturers

This rare and unboxed but perfect Robot from the late 1950s features an unusual illuminated colour television which portrays pictures from outer space; £250

·AIRFIX· ·INDUSTRIES·

Founded in England by Ralph Ehrmann and famous for its large range of plastic model construction kits made from the 1950s up to the present. The majority of Airfix kits were sold in the United Kingdom through F. W. Woolworth. They also made plastic figures and soldiers. It was reported in the *Daily Mail* newspaper in March 1964 that one million plastic US Marine Corps soldiers had been ordered for the Japanese market and 500,000 Arab figures for the Israeli market!

In 1971 Airfix Industries bought Meccano-Triang Ltd and continued to issue Dinky toys from the Binns Road factory in Liverpool. However, Airfix Industries ws forced to close down all its operations in 1979 including Dinky and was bought by Kenner-Parker. During the early 1980s Airfix was sold to the paint makers Humbrol Ltd of Marfleet, Hull.

Trademark

Airfix

·ALPS·LTD·

Founded in 1948 in Tokyo, Japan. They made a large range of tinplate clockwork and battery-operated toys.

Trademark

Mountain logo and 'Alps'.

·ARNOLD· ·COMPANY·

Founded in 1906 by Karl Arnold and established in Nuremberg, Germany, Arnold Co. is recognised as inventing the sparking flint mechanism. Famous for well-made clockwork motorcycle toys during the 1930s, many of which

incorporated large headlamps lit by flint
and wheel mechanisms. Probably the
most famous Arnold motorcycle toy is
'Mac', made in the early 1950s. Arnold
Co. also made an interesting selection of
boats before and after World War II.
Arnold continued to make ingenious
clockwork toys up until the 1960s. The
artwork used on Arnold Co. toys is most
distinctive and rather similar in style to
that of the French artist Toulouse-
Lautrec.
Trademarks
Arnold, Rapido

·ASAHI·TOY· ·COMPANY·

Founded in 1950 in Tokyo, Japan, and
manufacturers of a range of tinplate
novelty toys.
Trademark
Santa Claus carrying a sack marked
A.T.C.

·ASEKUSA· ·TOY·LTD·

Founded in 1950 in Tokyo, Japan;
concentrated on a range of highly
coloured tinplate novelty toys.
Trademark
A dog's face wearing a crown and
containing the letters A.I.

· BANDAI ·

Founded in 1950 in Tokyo, Japan, and most famous for a superb range of large-scale battery-operated toys including American saloons and robots. They still produce excellent plastic model kits of vintage vehicles.
Trademark
Gothic-style B with a C.

· BASSETT- · · LOWKE · LTD ·

Founded in 1899 in Northampton by W. J. Bassett-Lowke. During the company's formative years they worked closely with Bing and Carette, often importing German toy train parts into England. By the 1920s Bassett-Lowke was well established in its own right making accurately scaled model trains and boats. Bassett-Lowke products were always intended to be 'models' and as such do not fall within the realm of this publication.
Trademark
Lowko.

· BENBROS ·

Founded in 1952 by Jack and Nathaniel Benson at Gosport Road in Walthamstow, London. Initially Benbros made a range of necessities, including contraceptives, but entered the world of toy making with lead figures. They acquired four diecasting machines and began to make diecast toys similar in size and design to those made by Lesney Products. In fact, Benbros is believed to have made the horses for the large Lesney Coronation Coach. Benbros also made a direct copy of the smaller Lesney Coach. During the late 1950s Benbros made a range of

The poor quality of the TV series from Benbros contributed to their failure to compete with Lesneys miniatures. Strictly for fanatics; £7 each boxed

Old figures of Santa are always collectable and this, dating from 1954, is executed to a good standard; £125 boxed

diecast miniature models called the TV Series range. This range was later called 'Mighty Midgets'. Benbros also made Zebra Toys – larger-sized diecast vehicles. Benbros ceased production in the late 1960s.

Trademarks

Benbros, TV Series, Mighty Midgets, Zebra Toys.

· BING ·

Founded by Ignor and Adolf Bing in the mid-1860s and based at Nuremberg, Germany. The company made a vast range of boats, clockwork figures,

These tinplate models were designed for use as accessories, to be driven by model steam engines. Beautifully made and decorated, they typify the high standards of German tinsmithery in the 1920s; £60 each

steam-driven models, trains and cars. Bing products up to 1918 were marked 'GBN' (Gebrüder Bing, Nuremberg) whereas after 1919 they were marked 'BW' (Bing Werke). Due to the economic depression of the late 1920s the Bing works were forced into receivership in 1932. The toy boat business was taken over by Fleishmann and the rest of the Bing empire went to Bub.

Trademarks
GBN, BW.

· BLOMER · & · · SCHULER ·

Founded after World War I and manufacturers of a range of brightly coloured tinplate clockwork novelty toys. The company continued after World War II with many of their toys being made in the US Zone of Germany. Lesney Products based their tinplate elephant made in 1951 on the Blomer & Schuler toy. The company continued to make good quality tinplate novelty toys until 1971 when it closed.

Trademark
An elephant incorporating letters B & S.

Blomer and Schuler is a less well known toy manufacturer that adhered to traditional materials. This Merry-Go-Round was made in the 1960s; £25. The Turkey and Elephant are from 1948; £95 each

· BONNET ·
· ET · CIE ·

Bonnet Et Cie was founded in 1912 and was taken over by the Martin company, also based in Paris, in the early 1920s. Bonnet toys are very well made and in many cases were comparable in quality to their German rivals.

Trademarks

VEBE, V.B., VEB, VB et cie.

A rare and exquisitely made Auto Transporter by this French company represents the upper end of tin toy collecting; at least £500 boxed

· BRIMTOY ·
· (WELLS) · LTD ·

The firm of Wells began making toys just after World War I and manufactured inexpensive tinplate clockwork train sets and road-going vehicles. Wells took over the London-based Brimtoy Ltd in 1932. The company also made a small range of four poorly designed diecast cars which were

The Welsotoys Milk Float is a clever toy: when it stops and starts the sign on top of the float rises and falls; £60

Although not known for toys of the highest quality, Brimtoys are very appealing. This Searchlight Lorry from the 1930s is very rare in this condition; £250 boxed.

fitted with tin baseplates. The range of cars all fitted with clockwork mechanisms were made between 1946 and 1950. They are not particularly sought after and do not command high prices. Other Brimtoy Pocketoys included tinplate buses and trolley buses, commercial vehicles based on a Bedford cab made from a combination of tin, diecast and even plastic. Pocketoys were all mechanised in either of two ways – a clockwork motor or friction-operated motor. Brimtoy Pocketoys eventually ended up being made entirely out of plastic – a good example being the green Morris Minor car.

Trademarks

Nelson's Column (Brimtoys); two water wells (Wells O'London).

The tinplate Trolley Bus exhibits a high standard of decoration; £80

·W.BRITAINS· ·LTD·

Founded during the mid-19th century in London, the firm was eventually located in Birmingham. Although they made many clever working models, figures and games during their early years, it was their move into lead figures in 1893 that made them a household name. In fact, the name Britains is synonymous with lead soldiers. They also made farm and zoo sets, and a good range of military items, many of which

The one-ton Army Lorry is composed entirely of lead and is quite fragile; £75. The Tractor is worth £45. Both date from the 1940s

The Village Idiot is a rare and collectable piece—probably the rarest of all the farm series; £120. Although the farm equipment looks sturdy, it is not; £60

were fitted with clockwork motors and made in heavy diecast. Realising that plastic was becoming more and more popular, Britains Ltd acquired an interest in a local company of plastic figure manufacturers, Herald Miniatures, in 1954. By 1959 the two companies had fully merged and all products in plastic were sold as Britains. Famous ranges such as Swoppets, Eyes Right and Deetail were produced in the 1960s and 1970s. Britains also produced a range of OO gauge figures, animals and vehicles under the brand name of Lilliput. W. Britains Ltd is still in existence today and continues to make vast ranges of metal and plastic figures.

Trademarks

W. Britains, Swoppets, Deetail, Lilliput.

· BUB ·

The Karl Bub Company was founded in 1851 in Nuremberg, Germany. The company is most famous for its range of tinplate model trains both clockwork and electric. Bub took over Bing in 1933. After World War II they had a factory in England. Eventually the company ceased trading in 1967.

Trademark

Bub

Karl Bub—not well known in the UK—was a prolific manufacturer of trains. This set was produced in the mid-1950s; £150 boxed

· CARETTE ·

Founded in 1886 by Georges Carette in Nuremberg, Germany. Regarded as one of the top toy manufacturers and turned out the highest quality of tinsmithery. Many of his toys such as large-scale cars, boats and trains were hand-enamelled. Unique features of early Carette cars were folding windscreens and handbrakes. The Carette Company had ties with both Bing and Bassett-Lowke and Carette supplied both companies with railway carriages and locomotives. Carette closed in 1917, during World War I, and did not start up again until after the cessation of hostilities.
Trademarks
GC; GC & Cie.

Carette—a highly regarded maker of tin toys. This boat, made before 1914, was designed to emulate the movement of a ship when rolled across a floor. This toy was made in several sizes, this being a small version; £120

· CHAD · VALLEY ·

This famous British toy company was founded in the Chad Valley district of Birmingham in 1860 by Joseph and Alfred Johnson. In 1897 they moved to Harborne and began to establish a reputation for well-made, attractive and interesting traditional children's games and board games. During the 1930s Chad Valley began to develop and produce 'low quality' tinplate toys. Many of their tinplate novelty toys were based on the ever-popular Lehmann

The constructional Saloon Car dates from 1947; £65

Chad Valley: This cheaply made toy of simple construction is valuable purely because of the excellence of its lithographic decoration. Very few Chad Valley products are collectable; £230

toys that had been imported from Germany. The Chad Valley range was extended to include clockwork tinplate buses, saloons and commercial vans. Their best-known van is the Chad Valley Board Game Van – used not only as a toy but also as an advertisement – all the illustrated games were Chad Valley games! A short-lived range of construction toys known as Ubilda were also made during the 1930s. Chad Valley also made soft toys including teddy bears. One of their best designers, Norah Wellings, left Chad Valley in the 1920s to form her own (and later better-known) soft toy firm. After World War II Chad Valley turned some of their production capacity to diecast cars. In 1949 Chad Valley released a small range of diecast cars which were sold in part through the Rootes Group (famous for such cars as Hillman, Sunbeam Talbot and Humber). Although of value, these Chad Valley cars do not turn up that often and have a small specialist following of collectors. This range was discontinued by 1954 and Chad Valley concentrated on their board games which had always been packaged in boxes whose artwork reflected a 1920s feel. In the 1960s Chad Valley tried to update the style, suffered poor sales,

and reverted back to the old design.
Trademarks
Chad Valley Co. Ltd; Ubilda.

· CHARBENS ·

Founded by Charles and Benjamin Reid
in the late 1920s and manufacturers of
unsophisticated diecast toys in a factory
in Holloway, London. In 1955 in direct
competition to Lesney and to a lesser
extent Benbros, Charbens released their
'Old Crocks' range of miniature vintage
vehicles. They were never popular –
many of them suffered from a form of
metal fatigue. Production ceased during
the early 1960s.
Trademark
Old Crocks.

This obscure range of
vintage cars was produced
in the 1950s by Charbens.
Their only attribute is their
charming crudeness; at
the very most £10 boxed

· COMPAGNIE ·
· INDUSTRIELLE ·
· du JOUET ·

A French company based in Paris.
Founded in the early 1920s, the
company made high quality large-scale

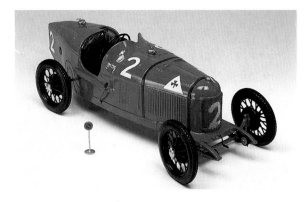

This C.I.J. model of an Alfa Romeo P2, made to an accurate scale, is recognised as being one of the all-time classic toy cars. Highly sought after, this particular example has been restored; £750; £3,000 if mint and boxed

The Magic Roundabout train is a rare and sought after item that still turns up very cheaply at boot fairs. It dates from 1970; £35 boxed

clockwork cars including the Alfa Romeo P2 (just under 22 inches in length). Mint boxed examples of this car fetch at auction over £2000.
Trademark
CIJ.

·CORGI·TOYS·

When Mettoy went into receivership in 1983 a successful management buy-out took place assisted by a leading financial institution called Electra Trust Plc. The new company of Corgi Toys continued to produce diecast toys for the Swansea-based factory. Although the standard range continued much as before, Corgi Toys identified a strong collectors' base and began to produce model vehicles

with relatively low production runs. Although some models did appreciate quickly, the strategy was plagued with difficulties, including toy wholesalers 'dumping' so-called valuable models onto the market at prices well below cost. In late 1989 Mattel Inc., the large American toy company, bought Corgi Toys.

Trademark
Corgi Toys.

· COWAN · · DE · GROOT ·

A British toy wholesaler and distributor founded by S. D. Cowan who were also world distributors of the John Bull printing outfits. They were also the proprietor of 'Codeg' toys which were made by toy manufacturers to their order, such as the 1964 Doctor Who dalek in both metal and plastic, and very cheap tinplate saloon cars. In the early 1960s the company diversified into electrical goods and appliances.

Trademark
Codeg.

· CRAGSTAN ·

Founded in the USA as a toy distributor only and not a producer during the 1950s. Their main source was the many good Japanese toy manufacturers whose products were imported into the USA. Cragstan often had their trademark imprinted on toys especially when they had sole distribution rights.

Trademark
Cragstan.

The Green Astronaut is a rare piece dating from the late 1950s and even with its missing antennae is still worth £300 unboxed

Cragstan, a prolific manufacturer, produced many of the Japanese battery toys which are now becoming very collectable. This Ford Thunderbird from 1965 features a power-operated convertible roof as well as rear wheel drive and steering; £125 boxed

C

· CRESCENT ·

The Crescent Toy Company was founded in the early 1920s and was based in London. During the period leading up to World War II they manufactured hollow cast lead figures and soldiers – these were less sophisticated than the products of W. Britains Ltd. After the war Crescent turned away from manufacturing to toy distribution. A good relationship was established with Die Casting Machine Tools Ltd (DCMT) who produced for Crescent a large range of diecast vehicles. These included fire engines, petrol tankers, a Jaguar saloon and Jaguar Police Car. They were rather badly designed in comparison with a Dinky diecast model. Although of some general interest today they do not command high prices. In 1949 Crescent opened their own factory in South Wales. They severed their arrangement with DCMT and began to make their own diecast models. Their most famous series was a range of ten Grand Prix racing cars made between 1956 and 1959. These racing cars are very collectable – the scarcest one being the Vanwall Racing Car.

Trademark
Crescent.

· DIE · CASTING ·
· MACHINE ·
· TOOLS ·

Known as DCMT, this London-based diecast manufacturer was founded just before World War II by Aubrey Mills and Sidney Ambridge. Jack Odell (see Lesney) was to serve his apprenticeship under Ambridge. After the war DCMT began to make a range of model vehicles for the Crescent Toy Company. At the same time DCMT developed their own range of toys under the Lone Star brand name. Toy guns and diecast train sets were successfully made during the 1950s and 1960s.
Trademark
DCMT.

· DISTLER ·

Founded at the turn of the century by Johann Distler in Nuremberg, Germany. Although better known for a superb range of highly collectable penny toys, Distler also made large-scale clockwork tinplate cars and trains during the 1930s. The company was eventually taken over by Trix.
Trademark
Distler.

The German manufacturer Distler always produced high quality toys. This attractive tinplate Sports Car was made in the 1940s; £290

· EINFALT ·

Founded in 1922 by Georg and Johann Einfalt in Nuremberg, Germany, this company made a large range of novelty toys but were most famous for their big tinplate toys using rail, cables or roadways. The company continued to produce these toys after World War II.
Trademarks
G.E.N.; Technofix (after 1935).

· ERTL ·

Ertl was founded by Fred Ertl in Dubuque, Iowa, USA, in 1945. Following the war Fred Ertl found himself out of work and started up in the business of making metal toy tractors at his home. In 1946 the firm was given the contract to produce toy tractors for John Deere, the giant farm equipment company. In 1947 Fred Ertl incorporated his business and by 1949 was producing 5000 toys a day. In 1959 the company moved to Dyersville, Iowa, and Ertl expanded their line into trucks and other toy vehicles. In 1967 the company was acquired by the Victor Comptometer Corporation. Ertl expanded its toy range further – plastic model kits were added in 1972 and in 1974 trucks under the Structo brand name. Victor was itself acquired by one of America's largest toy companies, Walter Kidd & Co., in 1977. In 1983 Ertl purchased the AMT division of Lesney Products. AMT products soon became merged with the Ertl model kit line. In 1987 Kidde Inc. merged with the Hanson Trust Ltd. In recent years Ertl have successfully acquired the licensing rights to many television, film and comic strip characters such as Noddy, Batman, Thomas the Tank Engine and Postman Pat.
Trademark
Ertl.

Three Ertl examples of collectable character toys. Ones to watch for in the future but currently widely available at normal retail selling prices

f

· FLEISHMANN ·

Founded in 1887 in Nuremberg, Germany. Famous for tinplate boats and magnetic floating toys. Fleishmann took over the Bing works boat business in 1932.

Trademark
GFN in a triangle.

Tinplate ships are amongst the rarest and most valuable of all collectable toys. This example is by Fleishmann, who are perhaps better known for their railway models; £350 even though its lifeboats are missing

· GILBERT · & · · COMPANY ·

Founded in 1909 in Connecticut, USA, by A.C. Gilbert who made a series of construction sets similar to Meccano, and a range of conjuring and magic sets.
Trademark
Erector.

Gilbert & Co. A famous American manufacturer whose products are not familiar in the UK. This Construction Car typifies the sturdiness that American manufacturers are known for. Parts of this example are made from pressed steel. It dates from the 1930s; £250

· (J.&H.) · · GLASMAN · · LTD ·

A firm of toy factors and distributors who ran their business from London during the 1940s and 1950s. They generally handled only the lower end of the range and often produced their own boxes for the toys which varied from diecast cars to small tinplate buses.
Trademark
Betal.

· GUNTHERMANN ·

Founded in 1877 in Nuremberg, Germany, by Siegfried Gunthermann, who died in 1890. His widow married Adolf Wiegel, whose initials were included in Gunthermann trademarks until 1919, thereafter SG was used. Gunthermann are famous for their well-made tinplate horse-drawn vehicles, fire engines and aeroplanes.
Trademarks
SG, AW.

A worn example of a tinplate Fire Engine from Guntermann. In this distressed condition it is worth £150

· HAUSSER ·

Founded in 1904 in Germany. Best known for a large range of composition figures sold under the trade name Elastolin. These figures were also used by toy manufacturers to add realism to their own products. Hausser also made tinplate military vehicles. Tin toy production had virtually ceased by the mid-1950s.

Trademarks

OMHL in a diamond; large A under sloping roof in a circle; Elastolin.

This Horse-Drawn Ambulance, dating from the 1920s, is a well preserved example by Hausser, who are perhaps better known for their Elastolin soldiers. Although two figures are missing, it is worth £175 unboxed

· HILL ·

The John Hill Co. (Johillco) was established at the turn of the century in London by an ex-employee of W. Britains Ltd. The company made hollow-cast type figures, both military and civilian, and coronation coaches. They have in recent times become highly collectable, although they do not command such high prices as for example Britains products.

Trademark

Johillco.

· ICHIKO · CO ·

Founded in post-war Japan and specialists in tin toys, especially cars. For example, the company made a large-scaled (24-inch) Mercedes Benz 300 SE in the 1960s. Collectors should be aware that this toy was reissued in the early 1980s, selling for £125.
Trademark
PW.

· JOUETS · de · · STRASBOURG ·

Founded in 1935 in Strasbourg, France, by G. Marx, and producers of an extensive range of mechanical tinplate toys.
Trademark
Joustra.

Jouets de Strasburg's products are rare in the UK but worth collecting. This car from the 1950s is typical of its time; £75

· KELLERMANN ·
· & · CO ·

Founded by Georg Kellermann in 1910 in Nuremberg, Germany, and specialists in inexpensive simple mechanical toys and penny toys.
Trademarks
CKO; KCO.

· KOHNSTAM ·

Moses Kohnstam founded his company of toy distributors and wholesalers in 1875 in Furth, Germany. Many of the local toy manufacturers used him to market and sell their toys and often the Kohnstam trademark was put on such toys. In the 1930s the Kohnstam family moved to England. After the war Richard Kohnstam, the grandson of Moses, continued the business of toy manufacturing and wholesaling the products of small London-based

This fine Police Car with radio and working searchlight, from a successful agent for imported toys, still bears its original price tag and dates from the 1920s; £400

companies such as Benbros and Lesney. There is a small range of diecast toys made by unknown manufacturers but all of which have the Khonstam trademark. These are of special interest to Matchbox collectors. Richard Kohnstam did much to promote the Lesney 'Machbox' Series, partly because he and not Lesney had registered the name 'Matchbox'. In 1959 Lesney bought out Richard Kohnstam.
Trademark
MOKO.

These three diecast toys were distributed with some success in the 1950s and in this condition are worth £60 each

· LEGO ·

In 1932 Gotfried Christiansen joined his father's carpentry business. He was technically minded and saw his future as a designer and manufacturer of 'clever' children's toys. The now world-famous brand name of Lego was registered in 1934. Lego in the Danish language basically means 'play-well'. Early Lego toys included wooden animals on wheels and a range of wooden cars, trains and planes. All such toys were rubber-stamped 'Lego'. After the war the firm began to experiment with plastic and introduced a range of toys that would today be called early learning or pre-school toys. Around 1948 they introduced their plastic interlocking toy bricks which have since changed very little in design.

During the 1950s and 1960s Lego also made boxed sets of plastic cars, petrol tankers and commercial vehicles which added realism to the buildings and roadways. These are eagerly sought after today by collectors. It is unlikely that Lego toy bricks will ever be very collectable due to the amount made in any one year. However, early boxed sets are sought after. The Lego company has a permanent display of their early product at the famous Legoland Centre in Denmark.

Trademark
Lego.

· LEHMANN ·

Founded in 1881 in Brandenburg by Ernst Lehmann and regarded as one of the most famous producers of collectable tinplate novelty toys during the 1920s. After World War II Brandenburg was in East Germany and the Lehmann Company, under Ernst

The Climbing Monkey was evidently a big seller for the company. It was first manufactured in the 1930s, £85, and reintroduced by Lehmann in the 1950s; £45 boxed

Lehmann were famous for their comprehensive range of toys. This mechanical novelty dates back to 1916. It reveals the care and standard of decoration applied to the most basic products; £120

Lehmann's cousin, Johann Richter, was set up in West Germany near Nuremberg. The company continued to make tinplate novelty toys, some of which were based on their classic pre-war toys. Today the company makes a vast range of large-scale plastic and metal trains which are popular in Germany and the USA.

Trademarks

EPL; a bell-shaped metal press containing a 'C' or a combination of EPL.

· LESNEY ·
· PRODUCTS ·

Founded in 1947 in North London by Leslie Smith and Rodney Smith, who were joined by Jack Odell shortly after. Odell designed a range of large-scale toys including a Road Roller and Cement Mixer. Rodney Smith resigned

Before Lesney found the way forward with the Matchbox range, they made a series of larger scale models of which this is the best known. This very fine Massey Harris Tractor was, in part, a promotional model in 1954, and in this boxed condition is worth £300

from the company in 1950. The 'Matchbox' Series – a range of miniature diecast model vehicles – was launched in 1953. This was followed in 1965 by the Models of Yesteryear range. During the 1960s Lesney was exporting to over 120 countries and producing some five million toys a week. Jack Odell went into semi-retirement during the 1970s. The economic recession of the late 1970s and early 1980s forced Lesney to go into receivership. The receivers sold the company for £16.5 million to Mr David Yeh, the owner of Universal Toys, in 1982. A new company was created, Universal Matchbox, which has Matchbox Toys subsidiaries around the world.

Trademarks
Early toys Lesney; Matchbox from 1954.

Lesney were to produce the legendary Models of Yesteryear series in 1956. These three examples of saloons were made in huge quantities; £20 each boxed

· LINEMAR ·

Founded in Japan in 1950. Although they produced animated novelty toys they are better known as toy distributors and wholesalers.

Trademark
Linemar.

· LINES ·
· BROTHERS ·

The Lines family started making wooden toys in the early 1860s. The company of Lines Bros. was founded in 1919 in South London by three Lines brothers, Walter, Arthur and William. They are credited with forming one of the first-ever mass production lines and made rocking horses, dolls' houses, dolls' prams, cycles, scooters and large wooden pull-along engines. In 1925 they moved to a new factory in Merton, London. In the same year Lines Bros. bought up Hamleys Toy Shop in Regent Street, which afforded them an excellent retail outlet for Tri-ang toys. This trademark was registered in 1927 and is three lines forming a triangle.

During the 1920s they launched a range of children's pedal-powered cars and these continued to be made in differing styles and materials up until the 1960s. In fact, there was very little that Lines Bros. did not make! Factories were acquired or built in South Wales and Birmingham. In 1932 they registered the brand name Tri-ang

This Tri-ang Delivery Van is one of the series of rugged outdoor toys made both before and after the war. Because of their large size, many were kept outside and very few survive in good condition. An unusual but interesting series to collect; £120

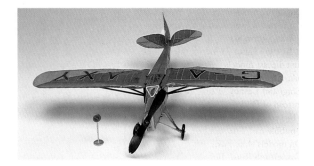

This Puss Moth flying model was marketed under the name Frog but was part of the Lines Group. These elderly models, by necessity constructed of the lightest possible materials, are rare today as many inevitably crashed; £55

Minic – a superb range of tinplate clockwork vehicles and buses. During the 1930s and 1940s Tri-ang continued to develop, famous brand names being Pedigree dolls and Frog model aircraft, the latter being made by a Lines subsidiary – International Model Ltd – at the Merton factory.

During the 1950s, most of the income for Lines Bros. was derived from their ever-successful children's pram side of the business. However, they also made large-scale pressed metal toys including buses, lorries and vans.

Tri-ang bought out Models Mini Ltd who made Scalex and Startex models. Scalex models had been fitted with a 12-volt electric motor and ran on track. Tri-ang developed the idea. The Tri-

This Tri-ang Gyro-Cycle being unusual and ingenious in design, is a favourite with toy collectors. A great many were produced but few survive in this condition from 1938; £80

ang racing cars were made in plastic and the brand of Scalextric was launched shortly afterwards.

In 1959 Lines Bros. introduced their first diecast models under the brand name Spot-On to compete with Dinky, Corgi and Lesney. A scale of 1/42 instead of Dinky's 1/43 was used so that a bus could stand comfortably alongside a bubble car! The vast majority of Spot-On models were made at the Castlereagh Road, Belfast, Northern Ireland, factory. Production of Spot-On models in Northern Ireland ceased in 1969. The production facilities were transferred to New Zealand and the range continued until 1972.

By the early 1960s Lines Bros. had acquired the Rovex train line – they supplied Marks & Spencer with rails and engines and by 1964 this side of the business accounted for more than one-third of Lines Bros.' profits.

During the mid-1960s Walter Lines who, as president of Tri-ang was possibly the world's largest toy maker, developed 40 wooden toys. Although faced with their own economic problems in 1964, Lines Bros. paid a sum of £800,000 for Meccano Ltd. Dinky toys continued to be made at Binn's Road, Liverpool. In 1970 the company became known as Meccano–Tri-ang Ltd and within one year had gone into receivership. Airfix Industries Ltd then bought the company but by 1979 this company had been forced to sell out to Kenner-Parker. The brand of Scalextric was sold to Hornby Hobbies.
Trademarks
Tri-ang; Spot-On;
Pedigree.

Lines were the largest manufacturers of pedal cars through several decades. This pressed steel car dates from 1961. Collectors should ensure they have the space to store and display pedal cars. Not overly collected, this example is worth £60

m

· MARTIN ·

One of the most famous French toy makers. The company was based in Paris and was founded by Fernand Martin in 1878. Their excellent tinsmithery rivalled many of the contemporary German toys. The majority of Martin toys were decorated by hand and were fitted with clockwork mechanisms. The company was taken over by Victor Bonnet & Co. in the early 1920s.
Trademark
FM within a circle.

Less well known in the UK, Martin, a French company, produced a Station Porter very similar in form to that of Lehmann's. This rather distressed version dates back to 1912; £120

· MARX ·

Founded in 1920 in New York, USA, by Louis Marx and by the 1960s rivalled Lines Bros. as being the world's largest toy manufacturer. Marx products were often aimed at the lower end of the market and were popular, amusing and cheap. A factory was opened in South Wales during the 1930s. After World War II the production of the

This Marx Batcraft from 1964 appeals mainly to character toy collectors. The same is true of this 'Launching Station'; £50 each

majority of Marx toys moved to the Far East. David Yeh, the present owner of Matchbox Toys, served his toy apprenticeship under the personal tutorage of Louis Marx in the 1950s. During the 1960s Marx toys were predominantly made from plastic.
Trademarks
Marx; Marlines.

· MATCHBOX ·
· TOYS ·

This company, a subsidiary of the Universal Matchbox Group, was formed in 1982 to replace Lesney Products, the latter company having been sold to Mr David Yeh, the founder of Universal Toys. Most of the famous Lesney brands have been continued, including Models of Yesteryear. In 1987 Matchbox purchased the Dinky brand name and launched a new range of Dinkys in 1988/9. Although the manufacturing side of the company was shifted to the Far East in 1985 the research and development of future

These recent commercial vehicles from Matchbox have an ardent collector following. The Texaco Tanker from 1989 can still be bought from toyshops; £5. The Lipton's Tea Van was introduced in 1977; £15 boxed.

models continues to be handled by
Matchbox Toys Ltd in Enfield,
Middlesex. Other Matchbox
subsidiaries can be found in West
Germany, Australia and the USA.
Trademark
Matchbox

· MATTEL · INC ·

Founded in California in 1945 as a small
doll-making company, during the late
1950s Mattel introduced to American
children the now internationally famous
teenage girl doll, Barbie. Children were
encouraged to play with their Barbie
dolls by the introduction of fashionable
outfits and other accessories such as
ponies, skis and ballgowns. Mattel Inc.
also made diecast toys – their range was
developed during the 1960s. In 1968
they registered the trademark 'Hot
Wheels' which was a revolutionary axle
and wheels which enabled the miniature
diecast car to move much quicker than,
for example, the Lesney Matchbox
Series. Lesney, who had been exporting
about 70 per cent of their products to
the USA in 1968, lost much of the
market to Mattel and never really
recovered. Mattel Inc. have now
become one of the largest toy
manufacturers in the world, with
operating plants in the Far East and
even England (Mattel have a subsidiary
company in England called Rosebud
Ltd). In 1989 Mattel Inc. bought out
Corgi Toys of Swansea, South Wales.
Trademarks
Mattel; Hot Wheels; Barbie; Rosebud.

· MECCANO ·

This famous British company was
founded by Frank Hornby at the turn of
the century. His first product was the

famous Meccano construction kit which was to span the world in unrivalled popularity for six decades. The success of this product was in part due to its flexibility which meant that a young child could make a recognisable model from just a few pieces, whilst at the other end of the scale an amateur engineer could produce an extremely sophisticated working model of practically anything.

Frank Hornby went on to produce a superb and comprehensive range of clockwork and, later, electric trains. These models were to break the domination of imported German manufacturers and were in reality just as well engineered but at a cheaper price than their rivals.

Shortly before his death Hornby produced a small range of diecast vehicles and figures intended to serve as lineside accessories, but these were quickly to have a life of their own and were, of course, to become the Dinky Toy range.

In 1937 Meccano launched a new series of model trains but to a smaller OO scale, and nearly all were to be electrically powered.

Dinky toy production from 1945 to 1964 is today regarded as the 'golden age' as far as collectors are concerned and they remained the mainstay of the company's fortunes.

In 1964, having perhaps failed to meet the challenge posed by Corgi and Lesney in this area, they were taken over by Tri-ang. Dinky toys ceased with the demise of Meccano in 1979.

Trademark
Meccano.

The British company Merrythought has an enviable reputation for the production of good quality teddy bears and other soft toys. This Teddy dates back to 1950; £25

· MERRYTHOUGHT ·
· LTD ·

Founded in 1930 by H. Janisch and C. Randle at Ironbridge in Telford, Shropshire. Although Merrythought made a large range of dolls, toys and games, they have become better known for their beautifully made teddy bears. Merrythought Ltd is still in existence today.

Trademark
Merrythought.

· METTOY ·
· COMPANY ·

Founded by Philipp Ullmann and Arthur Katz between 1934 and 1936 in Northampton. Ullmann had founded the Tipp Company in Germany in 1912 and had been joined there by Katz.

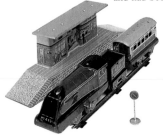

Mettoy, a comprehensive producer of toys, became best known for the introduction of Corgi Toys. This tinplate Train Set is typical of their pre-Corgi years; £75

Both were forced to flee Nazi Germany in 1934 due to their religion, and took up factory space with a firm of Northampton-based engineers. They developed a range of tinplate toys and opened their own factory in 1936. They launched the Mettoy company in the same year. The name derived from their product – metal toys.

Trademarks

Mettoys; Mettoy Playthings; Mettoy Playcraft.

·MODELS· ·MINI·LTD·

A small toy/model manufacturer originally of London and later Havant, Hampshire. The firm set up in 1947 and produced two obscure brands of tinplate cars – Scalex and Startex. They have in recent times become collectable not only by tinplate collectors but also by slot car enthusiasts because Scalex was the original 'Scalextric'. In total, ten cars were made. However, each car was issued in different colours, which makes it a complete but interesting range of cars to collect. Early Scalex models such as the Austin Healey or Jaguar 2.4 Saloon were fitted with clockwork mechanisms. In 1956 the clockwork motor was replaced by an electric 12-volt motor and a slotted track was made. Tri-ang liked the idea and bought out Models Mini Ltd in 1958. The Startex range was launched in the mid-1950s – a cord pull operated a mechanism inside the car. Only three cars were made under the Startex brand name: a Jaguar 2.4, an Austin Healey 100/6 and a Sunbeam Alpine Sports Car. Although missing parts such as steering wheels and windscreens (these were fitted to the Startex models) will affect the value, they are still of value to collectors. Any

one of the Mini Model range in mint/
boxed condition will be worth at least
£45 to £50.

Models Mini continued to produce
several toys for Tri-ang – many in
plastic, a popular example being a large
Wild West Chequers board game which
contained four dozen plastic cowboy and
indian figures.

Trademarks
Scalex; Startex.

· MODERN ·
· TOYS · (MT) ·

Founded by K. Masutoku in Tokyo,
Japan, in the early 1920s. This company
produced a vast range of toys often
using a combination of tin and celluloid.
During the 1950s and 1960s they made
ingenious battery-operated toys.

Trademark
TM within a diamond.

Modern Toys produced
many attractive toys of
which this 'Bubble Bear' is
a good example from the
late 1950s. £80 boxed

Morris and Stone produced many diecast toys but they were never to find fame in the way Matchbox did. This group of 'Esso' miniatures did not compare in quality with Lesney products; £10 each boxed

· MORRIS · & · · STONE · · (LONDON) · LTD ·

Founded by Morris and Stone just after World War II in North London. The company name was shortened to Morestone and they began making diecast toys similar in shape and size to those being made by Lesney. In 1954 Rodney Smith (a founder director of Lesney) joined Morestone and within a

The Davy Crockett Frontier Wagon is a good example of an early character toy; £20

year Morestone had launched a large range of diecast miniatures packaged in boxes resembling Esso petrol pumps. In 1960 Budgie Toys – 'they speak for themselves' – were introduced and shortly afterwards the company changed its name to Budgie Toys. In the early 1960s, Budgie was taken over by S. Guitermann but when faced with financial problems he in turn sold the company to Modern Products Ltd. Reproduction Budgie toys are being made today using the original tools.

Trademarks

Morestone; Budgie.

One of Morris and Stones most sought after vehicles is Supercar from the TV puppet series; £75

· PALITOY ·

This famous toy and doll company was originally known as Cascelloid Ltd, which was founded by A. E. Pallett in 1919. Early toys were made from plastic and celluloid. In 1937 Cascelloid Ltd was acquired by British Xylonite Ltd and moved to a new factory in Leicester. The range included a good range of character dolls including many Walt Disney figures. In 1966 Action Man was introduced, followed in 1971 by Action Girl. In 1968 the company was taken over by General Mills of America, a large food company. General Mills sold off Palitoy to Kenner-Parker in 1985, who did not use the name Palitoy on any of their products.
Trademark
Palitoy.

· PAYA ·

Undoubtedly the most famous Spanish tinplate toy manufacturer. Based in Alicante, the firm began to make tinplate toys in 1906. Many were fitted with clockwork motors. This range ceased in 1950 when production was

Spain is not normally thought of as a country with a heritage in toy production but Paya, based in Alicante, are now doing accurate reproductions of their old forgotten products. This fine Bugatti can be purchased from specialist outlets; £350

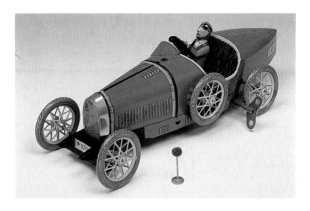

turned over to a cheaper range of toys incorporating a mixture of tin and plastic. In 1986 Paya decided to reissue many of their earlier vintage tinplate toys, using the original tools that had been stored safely. It was decided that these re-runs would be limited to 5000 of each model, after which the tools would be rendered inoperable and donated to the Spanish Historical Museum. These reissued toys have had a mixed reception. On the one hand they are beautiful tinplate toys and some of them are very reasonably priced. In fact, the range starts at £15 but unfortunately reaches £350 for the No. 970 1930-type Bugatti Racer. Others believe that they will not be 'good investments' because there are too many being made and because as they are being sold as collectors' pieces there will not be the natural wastage that would be associated with a tinplate toy from the 1930s. Already they have attracted a following of collectors who are buying them because they could never afford the prices asked for antique tinplate toys.

Trademark
PAYA.

· PEDIGREE · · SOFT · TOYS · · LTD ·

A subsidiary company of the Lines Bros. group which made good quality mass-produced plastic dolls at the Merton factory in London. In 1963 they introduced the Sindy Doll and a range of character toys including a Captain Scarlett doll. One such doll missing his hat sold for £160 at a specialist toy auction in 1990. In 1968 Rovex Industries Ltd took over Pedigree and production was moved to Canterbury in Kent. In 1978 Rovex and Pedigree were taken over by the Dunbee Combex Marx company which in 1980 was in turn taken over by Tamwade Ltd.

Trademark Pedigree.

Pedigree: a prolific manufacturer of dolls, this early plastic example dates from the 1960s; £35

p

· PELHAM ·
· PUPPETS ·

Founded in 1947 in Marlborough, Wiltshire, by Bob Pelham, and still in existence today, Pelham made an expansive range of hand-held puppets aimed solely at children. During the 1950s Pelham started a Pelham Puppets Club. Early puppets were made entirely from wood, whereas modern puppets feature moulded heads and faces. Pelham have liaised closely with film and television producers and have made many famous characters such as Pinocchio and Muppets under licence. Three Pelham puppets from the 'Mike Mercury' television series sold at a specialist toy auction in 1990 for £255.
Trademark
Pelham Puppets.

Pelham Puppets, the best known of puppet makers in the UK, have a very small collector following. Many puppets have survived and these two examples of this traditional toy from the 1950s are worth £25 boxed

· RANLITE ·

Ranlite model cars were moulded out of Bakelite – an early plastic – during the 1930s by a Halifax firm known as Automobiles (Geographical) Ltd. They are a true collectors' piece today as few were made and due to their fragile composition they were easily damaged. They are not true toys – they could easily be classified as models and to a certain extent as construction cars because they could be assembled by the purchaser. They were also very sophisticated – remote control was standard, the tyres were semi-pneumatic but they were expensive to buy. The same can be said of them today as a good example of a Singer or Austin car would be worth at least £200 to a collector – more would be paid for the Golden Arrow racing car introduced in 1931.

Trademark
Ranlite.

· SCALEXTRIC ·

Scalextric was created by Lines Bros. in 1958. At the same time Lines Bros. owned Meccano and Hornby. The growth in car ownership during the 1950s and 1960s, modern motorways and the popularity of motor racing created a keen demand for racing track layouts. The idea of electrified slot car racing had been developed by Models Mini Ltd who had successfully introduced their Scalex tinplate models in the mid-1950s. During the early 1960s Lines Bros., who at the time were the largest toy manufacturers in the world, ran an international grand prix for owners of Scalextric racing car sets.

In 1964 Scalextric sets started at just under £4 and offered the child 24 different plastic model cars and more than 50 buildings and accessories. Early Scalextric cars had detachable rubber compound drivers in two sizes. The racing cars always had the larger size and if missing greatly affect the value of such a car. The brand name was acquired as part of Hornby Hobbies in

Scalextric has been in existence since the 1950s and its product has endured where others have failed. These very early examples were made in tinplate. Although without their drivers, they are worth £35 each

the 1970s. Scalextric is just as popular today and has a large following of enthusiasts who are a mixture of 'runners' and collectors.

Trademark
Scalextric.

· SCHREYER ·
· & · CO. ·

Founded in 1912 in Germany by H. Mueller and H. Schreyer, although they traded under Schreyer & Co., it is their trademark Schuco that has become the more famous. Many collectors rate Schuco toys as the most technically advanced of their type. During the 1920s and 1930s they produced a vast range of novelty clockwork toys including animals that were wound up by an arm, leg or tail and not a key. After World War II the company also produced an inexpensive range of clockwork tinplate cars, some of which were the 'Steerable Driving School Car'

This Telesteering Car was supplied with obstacles around which it could be manoeuvred. It was clearly an effort to provide extra value for money by Schreyer & Co. The car dates from 1936; £80

Two further examples from Schreyer which have well-made clockwork motors to power the vehicle and to operate the horn. Dating from the 1930s; £75 each

and Test Steer, the former of which came with tools and a jack to remove the wheels and the latter with wooden pegs in which to test the child's skill in directing the car through the obstacles. The car was attached to a wire for direction. Schuco toys made in the immediate post-war era were marked as having been made in the US Zone of Germany. This period lasted until 1951. After that all their production was marked 'made in Germany' or words to that effect. Schuco went out of business in 1977 but Gama bought the brand name (a similar example is whereby Matchbox bought the Dinky name in 1987) and several early Schuco tinplate models from the Old Timer series such as the Schuco Examica 4001 were remade by TMX Toys, a subsidiary of Gama. Schreyer & Co. also made a range of toy and model aircraft – one good example seen is the Radiant 5600 which was liveried in many of the more famous civilian airlines such as Pan American, BOAC and Air France. Batteries were used to power the engines which would start up in sequence. The plane would taxi and move in a circle and then the engines would close down, once again in sequence. Aspiring tinplate aeroplane collectors should look to Schucos as being a relatively inexpensive way to start a tinplate collection.

Trademark
Schuco.

· STEIFF ·

Founded by Margaret Steiff in Grengen Brenz, Germany, in the late 1870s. She had begun making dolls for the local children, and when she realised how popular they were she began to expand the business. Steiff produced a catalogue in 1894 and from 1905 used the now famous hexagonal metal ear button as a trademark. By 1909, the year Margaret Steiff died, the company was advertising a vast range of soft and cuddly toys and dolls: bears, kangaroos, monkeys, clowns and a novelty figure known as Krackjack that had a large body, a pointed head and a wicked smile – all made from felt, plush and velvet and guaranteed not only to be indestructible but also to be a Steiff toy if it had the 'Button in the Ear'. The Steiff company still produces today a large range of soft toys including a collectors' range of famous Steiff bears.

Trademark
Hexagonal metal ear button.

· SUTCLIFFE ·
· PRESSINGS ·
· LTD ·

Founded in 1885 in Horsforth near
Leeds in Yorkshire, England, by the
early 1920s Sutcliffe was manufacturing
a good range of toy boats in both wood
and metal. The company closed down
in 1982.
Trademark
Sutcliffe.

Sutcliffe & Co., the famous
family concern, ceased
trading recently and left
behind a long legacy of toy
boat manufacture. This
Frigate 'The Grenville',
dates from the early
1940s; £50

· TIMPO · TOYS ·

This firm of Toy Importers Ltd was founded in London just before the outbreak of World War II. The range of Timpo toys included soft toys, wooden toys such as forts, heavy metal toys and figures. During the war the company made a small range of figures using a substance similar to Elastolin, i.e. sawdust and glue which when mixed together was moulded onto a wire frame and then hardened and painted. Unlike British toy firms, Timpo were able to continue manufacturing during the war. They introduced a rang of hollow-cast lead vehicles which were similar in design to the range made by Meccano Dinky.

The range of vehicles was expanded after the war but due to their crudeness and the ever-growing sophistication of Dinky they were discontinued at the end of the 1940s. The Timpo rang of figures, however, were very popular and varied from soldiers to cowboys and indians. Although they are not as collectable as W. Britains' products they do have their own small band of collectors.

Trademark
Timpo.

· TIPP · & · COMPANY ·

Founded in Nuremberg in 1912 by Tipp and Carstans, by 1919 Philipp Ullmann had succeeded as the sole owner of the company. During the 1930s this company made a good range of large-scale tinplate cars and aeroplanes. In 1934 Ullmann was forced to leave Nazi Germany and set up business in South Wales where the firm Tipp & Co. continued to produce

tinplate toys until 1971.
Trademark
T. Co. intertwined or Tippco.

· T.N. ·

The company Nomura Toys was
founded in Tokyo, Japan, in 1923. A
large range of tinplate clockwork novelty
and character toys were made in the
post-war period.
Trademark
T.N. within a diamond.

· TRIX ·

Founded in 1927 in Nuremberg,
Germany, and originally manufacturers
of good quality construction sets, Trix
had a business tie-in with Bassett-
Lowke. During the 1930s Trix took
over the Distler company. In 1935 Trix
showed the toy trade their Trix Express
set – an ingenious overhead electrified
train set. At the same time the company
left Nazi Germany and set up in

The products of Trix, the
German manufacturer, are
not avidly sought after by
collectors in the UK which
keeps prices down. This
1950s set is worth £100
boxed

Northampton, England. Production continued after the war, the most popular toy being the Trix Twin Railway System whereby two locomotives could be independently operated on the same electric track. Although Trix products made in England are collectable, by far the more collectable are the toys made in Germany.

Trademark

Trix.

· TOOTSIETOY ·

Based in Chicago, Tootsietoy was the diecast and toy manufacturer to the USA as Meccano Dinky was to Britain. Their first models were issued in 1910 and the company enjoyed their golden era during the 1930s and 1940s. Tootsietoy products were mainly sold in the USA. With relatively few exported, they are mainly collected in the USA and are seldom seen for sale in Britain.

Trademark

Tootsietoy.

· TOY · TIME · · TOYS · LTD ·

Established in 1937 by David Todd and based in Southport, Lancashire. Toy Time Toys made a large range of plastic dolls during the late 1940s and 1950s including sleeping dolls, walking dolls and many different types of black dolls. Toy Time Toys became Bluebell Dolls Ltd in 1969. In 1974 the company was taken over by Denys Fisher Toys.

Trademarks

Roddy, Rodnoid, Bluebell Dolls.

·VICTORY·
·INDUSTRIES·

A short-lived toy/model car manufacturer who traded as Electric Models, Victory Industries, Guildford, Surrey, during the early to mid-1950s. Victory made a superb range of large-scale (1/18) British saloon and sports cars including a Triumph TR2 open sports car. Most of their products were not aimed at children – in fact, most of their outlets were in garage showrooms. Victory Industries also made boats – one example being the Vosper RAF Crash Tender which was made in collaboration with Vosper Ltd in Portsmouth. A brief sortie into the development of slot cars resulted in a very well-made racing car set, comprising metal roadways/track and plastic sports cars. It is thought that the firm ceased in the late 1950s.
Trademark
Victory.

This racing car set by Victory from the late 1950s betrays an uncharacteristically amateurish approach in comparison to its rivals. Sets such as this are rare because they simply did not survive enthusiastic racing; £100

specialist services

The following are not definitive listings but published as a
guide and starting point for the new collector.

toy fairs and swapmeets

Over the last 20 years swapmeets have become one of the best sources for buying or selling obsolete collectable toys. They had humble beginnings – toys may have been for sale on one or two stalls at an antiques fair or there may have been a stall or two set up at a model train or diecast model club meeting to enable the members to do a little swapping. By the mid-1970s the popularity of toy collecting was beginning to gain momentum and the need for well-run swapmeets or toy fairs was recognised. Many of the earlier events took place in village halls or church halls. As the toy hobby became more sophisticated the better events in the early 1980s moved to leisure centres or racecourse stands. There are aproximately five different toy shows held each weekend in all parts of the country. The organisers often advertise in the local press. Below is a list of the recommended shows in alphabetical order and a contact number which could assist the collector in finding out the relevant dates for the calendar year:

- Buxton Toy Show   0335 42093
- Chester International Toy Show   0244 46297
- Farnham Maltings Toy Show   0276 681808
- Gloucester Toy Show   0242 524644
- Leeds Toy Show   0535 43825
- Sandown Toy Show   0858 62510
- Windsor Toy Show   0256 780170

You are encouraged to contact one of the organisers and take along with you some of your toys. Many of these events have in excess of 100 dealers, the majority of which will be happy to give a valuation and offer advice on your theme whether it be trains, dolls, tinplate or diecast models.

magazines

AIRFIX MAGAZINE 6 Crittall Road, Witham, Essex CM8 3BA.

ANTIQUE TOY WORLD Dale Kelley, 3941 Belle Plaine, Chicago, IL 60618, USA.

COLLECTORS FAYRE Quartet Publications, 149 North Street, Romford, Essex.

COLLECTORS GAZETTE 91 Kirkby Road, Sutton-in-Ashfield, Notts. NG17 1GH.

MODEL AUTO REVIEW MAR P.O. Box MT1, Leeds LS17 6TA.

MODEL COLLECTOR Link House Dingwall Avenue, Croydon CR9 2TA.

MODEL MART Castle House, 97 High Street, Colchester, Essex CO1 1TH.

shops

BOSCOMBE MODELS & COLLECTORS SHOP 802C Christchurch Road, Boscombe, Bournemouth (0202 38884). *Soldiers, lead toys, railways, planes, ships, tinplate etc.*

CHESTER TOY MUSEUM TOY SHOP 13A Lower Bridge Street Row, Chester CH1 1RS (0244 46297). *Matchbox, Dinky, Corgi, Hornby, tinplate etc.*

CLOCKWORK & STEAM 35 Western Street, Brighton (0273 203290). *Tinplate trains, Hornby, Bassett-Lowke lead figures, books etc.*

COLLECTORS OLD TOY SHOP 89 Northgate, Halifax, West Yorkshire (0422 360434). *Trains, soldiers, tinplate, novelty toys, ships etc.*

FRIZINGHALL MECCANO 202 Keighley Road, Frizinghall, Bradford BD9 4JZ (0274 542515). *Meccano, books etc.*

shops

J. & A. DIECASTS 139 Wyley Road, Radford, Coventry CV6 1NX (0203 396564). *Corgi, Dinky, Matchbox.*

MAGPIE MODELS & COLLECTORS SHOP 4 Regent Street, Chapel Allerton, Leeds LS7 4PE (0532 692617). *Britains, Dinky, Corgi, Matchbox etc.*

MW MODELS 4 Greys Road, Henley-on-Thames, Oxon RG9 1RY (0491 572436). *Meccano products etc.*

MICHAEL ROOUM Stand B13/A26 Grays Mews Antique Market, 1–7 Davies Mews, London (01 499 0482). *Dinky, Corgi, Matchbox, Spot-On, French Dinky etc.*

NOSTALGIA TOY MUSEUM COLLECTORS SHOP High Street, Godshill, Isle of Wight PO38 3HZ (0983 730055). *Matchbox, Dinky, Disneyania etc.*

PAST, PRESENT TOYS 862 Green Lane, Winchmore Hill, London N21 (01 364 1370). *Obsolete diecast, tinplate, trains, dolls etc.*

PETE McASKIE Stand D10–12, Basement, Grays Mews Antiques, 1–7 Davies Mews, London W1 (01 629 2813). *Tinplate, Dinky, Corgi, Matchbox, books etc.*

SETOCRAFT Stand Y2 and Y3 Antiquarius, 131–141 King's Road, London SW3. *Robots, character-related, space, Corgi, Dinky etc.*

TIME MACHINE 198 Holbrook Lane, Coventry (0203 663557). *Matchbox, Corgi, Dinky etc.*

TOY EMPORIUM 297 Tettenhall Road, Wolverhampton WV6 0LB (0902 752257). *Matchbox, Dinky, Corgi etc.*

VECTIS MODELS 96 High Street, Cowes, Isle of Wight PO31 7AW (0983 292272). *Dinky, Matchbox, Corgi, tinplate etc.*

clubs and associations

If you are interested in receiving more information most clubs will send details of membership and subscriptions on receipt of a large stamped addressed envelope.

· NATIONAL ·

CORGI COLLECTORS CLUB c/o Mrs Pownall, Kingsway, Swansea Industrial Estate, Fforestfach, Swansea SA5 4EL (0792 586223).

HORNBY ASSOCIATION c/o 2 Ravensmore Road, Sherwood, Nottingham NG10 5PA.

THE MATCHBOX INTERNATIONAL COLLECTORS ASSOCIATION 13A Lower Bridge Street Row, Chester CH1 1RS (0244 346297). *Matchbox toys from 1947 to date, Dinky etc.*

PLASTIC COLLECTORS CLUB c/o 'Plastic Warrior', 65 Walton Court, Woking, Surrey GU21 5EE. *Specialising in Britains Ltd plastic figures, soldiers etc.*

· LOCAL ·

COVENTRY DIECAST MODEL CLUB (0203 595963).

MAIDENHEAD STATIC MODEL CLUB (Ruislip 673386).

SOUTH ESSEX DIECAST MODEL CLUB (0268 26899).

SURREY DIECAST MODEL CLUB (0344 51724).

WESSEX MODEL & TOY COLLECTORS CLUB (Bristol 864596).

display cabinet makers

ACORN PRODUCTS Peter Daw, 14 Glenway, Glenwood, Bognor Regis, West Sussex PO22 8BO (0243 823415).

D.M.S. DISPLAY CABINETS 26 Pine Close, Great Bentley, Essex CO7 8NX (0206 251116).

D.S.C. SHOWCASES 42 Radcliffe Drive, Ipswich IP2 9QZ (0473 684425).

FALCON FRAMES & CABINETS Ian Garvie, Unit A21, Little Heath Industrial Estate, Old Church Road, Coventry (0203 685971).

HARTNIGS French Field Farm, Carleton, Penrith, Cumbria CA11 8UA (0768 62754).

MALCOLM UNWIN 36 Aster Road, Kempshott, Basingstoke, Hants RG22 5NG (0256 57449).

PICTURE PRIDE DISPLAYS 17 Willow Court, Crystal Drive, Sandwell Business Park, West Midlands (021 544 4946).

TIMBERCRAFT CABINETS 5 Duke Street, Northampton NN1 3BE (0604 231082).

TIMBERCRAFT NORTHWEST 9 Heights Road, Nelson, Lancs BB9 0QE (0282 62216).

toy and doll museums

ARUNDEL TOY & MILITARY MUSEUM 23 High Street, Arundel, West Sussex BN18 9AD (0903 882908). *Tinplate, trains, soldiers.*

BETHNAL GREEN MUSEUM OF CHILDHOOD Cambridge Heath Road, London E2 9PA (01 980 2415). *Traditional toys, trains, cars, soldiers, dolls' houses, dolls.*

CHESTER TOY & DOLL MUSEUM 13A Lower Bridge Street Row, Chester CH1 1RS (0244 346297). *Tinplate, trains, Dinky, Matchbox, dolls.*

COCKTHORPE HALL TOY MUSEUM Cockthorpe, Wells-Next-The-Sea, Norfolk (0328 75293). *Tinplate, trains, Meccano, dolls etc.*

LONDON TOY & MODEL MUSEUM 21 Craven Hill, London W2 3EN. *Tinplate, trains, dolls etc.*

MERLEY HOUSE MODEL MUSEUM Merley, Wimborne, Dorset. *Dinky, Corgi, Tri-ang, Matchbox etc.*

VINTAGE TOY & TRAIN MUSEUM Fields Department Store, Market Place, Sidmouth, Devon. *Meccano, Dinky, Hornby.*

index

Where an entry and illustration appear on the same page, the illustration has not been indexed separately.

Action Man, 167
aeroplanes,
  construction kits, 15–16, 40–1
  diecast, 12–14, 55–6
  tinplate, 10–12
  and see Airfix; Compagnie Industrielle du Jouet; Dinky; Fleishmann; Frog; Gunthermann; International Model Aircraft; Marx; Matchbox; Meccano; Mettoy; Schuco; T.N.
agricultural vehicles, 44, 53, 124, 135, 153 and see Britains
Airfix Industries Ltd, 15, 101, 128, 157
Alfa Romeo, 140
Alpine Express, 96
Alps Ltd, 128
ambulances, 85–6, 148
AMT, 101 and see Ertl
animal figures,
  battery-operated, 25–6, 26
  lead, 16–19
  plastic, 19–20
  tinplate, 20–1, 132
  wood/paper, 20, 21–2
  and see Blomer & Schuler; Britains; Hausser, Herald Miniatures; John Hill; Timpo
Antarctic Explorers, 20
Aquitania, 88
arks, 21–2, 22
Arnold Company, 32, 34, 95, 128–9
Arnotts van, 76, 78
Asahi Toy Company (ATC), 129
Asekusa Toy Ltd, 129
Aston Martin DB2-4 Mark I, 75
Aston Martin (James Bond), 32, 35, 46, 47, 48, 103
astronauts, 111–12, 142 and see space toys
ATC see Asahi Toy Company
Austin cars, 42, 61, 103, 163
Austin pedal cars, 99
automatons see battery toys
Automobiles (Geographical) Ltd, 171
Avenger Set, 46
Avro Vulcan, 13
Avro York, 13
AW see Gunthermann

Baby Wee, 30
Balky Mule, 93
Bandai, 130
banks, 23–4
Barbie, 160
Bassett-Lowke Ltd, 125–6, 130, 137, 178
Batman, 145
Batmobile, 36, 37, 47, 101
battery toys, 25–7
  animals, 25–6
  astronaut, 112
  cars, 25–6, 32, 33, 85, 102–3
  human figures, 25–6
  robots, 25, 104–5, 128
  and see electric toys; Alps; Bandai; Cragstan; Gama; Ichiko; Linemar; Modern Toys; Schreyer; T.N.
Beatles, 47
Bedford vans, 43, 61
Benbros, 51, 91–2, 130–1, 151
Bentley cars, 43, 46, 47, 77, 141
Betal see Glasman
Bing, 122, 125–6, 131–2, 136, 137
Bionic Woman, 39

Black Beauty, 47
Blomer & Schuler, 132
Bluebell Dolls Ltd, 178
Bluebird car, 34, 45
board games see Chad Valley; Models Mini
boats, 27–30, 137, 146
  and see Arnold Company; Bing; Carette; Fleishmann, Hornby; Sutcliffe Pressings; Tri-ang; Victory Industries
Boeing Stratocruiser, 14
Bond, James, Aston Martin, 32, 35, 46, 47, 48, 103
Bonnet et Cie, 133, 158
Boston, Wendy, golliwog, 72
Brimtoy (Wells) Ltd, 64–5, 133–4
Britains, W., Ltd, 135–6
  animal figures, 16–20
  character toys, 37–8
  coronation coaches, 50
  Disneyania, 64
  motorcycles, 92
  soldiers, 106–10, 111
Bru, 71
Bub, 126, 132, 136
Bubble Bear, 164
Buck Rogers, 38
Budgie Toys, 166 and see Morris & Stone
Bugatti, 167, 168
Buick, 87
Bulwark, 88
buses, 84
BW see Bing

Capstan Cigarettes van, 55
Captain Scarlet, 168
car transporters, 42, 44, 60–1, 133
cardboard toys, Disneyania games, 63
Carette, 125–6, 137
carousel, 95
cars,
  battery-operated, 25–6, 32, 33, 85, 102–3
  clockwork, 31, 32, 33, 34, 81–2, 139–40, 163
  construction kits, 40–1, 137, 147
  diecast, 33–5, 57–9, 138, 139, 143
  electric, 163
  pedal, 98–9, 155, 157
  plastic, 87–8, 171
  tinplate, 26, 31–3, 35–6, 83, 84, 144, 149, 163, 173–4
  and see Arnold; Bandai; Carette; Corgi; Dinky; Gunthermann; Lesney; Mangold; Matchbox; Paya; Schuco; Spot-On; Tipp; Tri-ang
Cascelloid Ltd see Palitoy
cast-iron toys, trains, 126
Castoys, 82
cement mixer, 74, 153
Chad Valley, 32, 137–9
character toys,
  diecast, 36–7, 45–7
  lead, 37–8
  plastic, 38–40
  tinplate, 35–6
  and see Bandai; Britains; Corgi; Dinky; Disneyania; Ertl; Fairylite; Gama; human figures; Kenner; Marx; Matchbox; Mattel; Morris & Stone; Palitoy
Charbens, 109, 139
Charlie Weaver, battery-operated toy, 26
Chevrolet Impala, 44
Chinese toy manufacture, 97
Chitty Chitty Bang Bang, 36–7, 47
Chrysler Airflow, 53
CIJ see Compagnie Industrielle du Jouet

index

circus vehicles, 45, *97*, *141*
CKO *see* Kellermann & Co
Climbing Monkey, *152*
clockwork toys, 81
  animals, 20–1
  boats, 27–30
  cars, 31, *32*, *33*, *34*, 81–2, 139–40, 163
  coronation coach, *50*, 51
  Disneyania, 64
  motorcycles, 89–90, 95
  trains, 119–20
  and see novelty toys; Alps; Arnold; Bing;
    Blomer & Schuler; Brimtoy (Wells);
    Britains; Bub; Chad Valley;
    Compagnie Industrielle du Jouet;
    Distler; Lines Brothers; Martin;
    Mettoy; Minic; Models Mini; Paya;
    Schreyer; T.N.
clubs and associations, 185
Coca-Cola van, *76*
Codeg *see* Cowan de Groot
Commer Refrigerator Truck, 43
commercial vehicles, 61, 78–9, 86–8, 124,
    159 and see delivery vans
Compagnie Industrielle du Jouet, 139–40
constructor kits, *11*, 15–16, 40–1, *137*, *147*
    and see Airfix; Bandai; Gilbert;
    Meccano
Corgi, *34*, 35, 36, 41–9, 82–3
Corgi Classics, 45, *46*, 49
Corgi Major, 43–4
Corgi Toys, 14, 49, 53, 140–1, 160 *and see*
    Mettoy Company
coronation coaches, 49–51, 74–5, 130 *and
    see* Benbros; Britains; John Hill;
    Lesney; Morris & Stone; Taylor &
    Barratt
Corvette, 101
Courtenay, W. T., 109
Cowan de Groot, 141
Cragstan, 112, 142
crane truck, 61
crash truck, 86–7
Crescent, 109, 143

Daiya, 112
Daktari Gift Set, 47
Daleks, 39, 102–3, 141
Dan Dare, 113
Dancing Couple, *94*
Davy Crockett Frontier Wagon, *165*
DCMT *see* Die Casting Machine Tools Ltd
Deans Rag Book Co, 72
Deetail, 110–11 *and see* Britains
delivery vans, 43, *52*, 61, 78–9
  Arnotts, *76*, 78
  Capstan Cigarettes, 55
  Coca-Cola, *76*
  Goblin Vacuum Cleaners, 79
  Lipton's Tea, 78–9, *159*
  Lyons Swiss Roll, *58*
  Macleans Toothpaste, 87–8
  Osram, 78
  Rice Krispies, *159*
  Royal Mail, 55
  Sunlight Soap, *76*
  and see commercial vehicles
Denys Fisher Toys, 39, 179
Die Casting Machine Tools Ltd (DCMT),
    143, 144
diecast toys,
  aeroplanes, 12–14, 55–6
  cars, 33–7, 41–9, 57–9, 138–9, 143
  characters, 36–7, 45–7
  coronation coaches, 50–1
  Disneyania, 63–4

motorcycles, 90–2
ships, 56–7, *88*, 88–9
soldiers, 50, 108
trains, 118–26
  and see Benbros; Brimtoy (Wells);
    Britains; Chad Valley; Charbens;
    Corgi; Crescent; Die Casting Machine
    Tools; Kohnstam; Lesney; Lines
    Brothers; Mattel; Morris & Stone;
    Spot-On; Tootsietoy
Dinky Toys, 52–61, 128, 159, 161
  advertising vans, 61
  aeroplanes, 12–14, 55–6
  cars, 33–4, 57–9
  military vehicles, 61
  motorcycles, 90
  ships, 56–7
  space toys, 112
  and see Matchbox; Meccano
Dinky Dublo, 124
Dinky Supertoys, 59–61
Disneyania, 62–5 *and see* character toys;
    Britains; Marx; Matchbox
display cabinets, 186
Distler, 144, 178
Doctor Who, 39, 102–3, 141
dolls, 60, 66–71, 160, 168, *169 and see*
    character toys; novelty toys; Pedigree
    Soft Toys; Steiff; Toy Time Toys
Donald Duck, 63
Drummer Clown, *95*
Duesenberg, 79

Einfalt, *92*, 94, *96*, 145
Elastolin toys, 21, 109, 148
Electric Models, 180
electric toys,
  cars, 163
  trains, 120
  and see battery toys; Bub; Scalextric;
    Trix; Victory Industries
elevator loader, 61
ELR (East London Rubber Co), 99
EPL *see* Lehmann
Erector *see* Gilbert & Company
Ertl, 145
Eton train, 122
Eyes Right *see* W. Britains Ltd

Fairylite, 39
farm animals *see* animal figures
farm equipment *see* agricultural vehicles
figures *see* animal figures; human figures
film related toys *see* character toys
fire engines, 77, 78, *82*, 143
Fleischmann, 132, 146
Flying Fortress, *13*
flying saucers, *113 and see* space toys
FM *see* Martin
Foden lorries, *58*, 59
Forbidden Planet, 104
Ford cars, *34*, 42–3, 44, 78, 103, *142*
Freddie Kreuger, 39–40
friction motors, 86
Frog, 15, 156

Gama, *14*, 174
games *see* Chad Valley; Disneyania; Models
    Mini
garages 86
GBN *see* Bing
GC/GC & Cie *see* Carette
G.E.N. *see* Einfalt
GFN *see* Fleishmann
Ghost Busters, 39
Gilbert & Company, 41, *147*

index

Glasman, J. & H., Ltd, 147
GMC van, 79
Goblin Vacuum Cleaner van, 79
Goebel doll, *70*
golliwogs, 72
Goofy, 38, 62
Green Hornets, 47
Gunthermann, *94*, 147
Gus and Jaq, *64*, 65
Gustav the Climbing Miller, *93*
Guy lorries, *58*
Gyro-Cycle, *156*

Hamleys Toy Shop, 155
Hank and Silver King, *38*
harbour sets, 88–9
Harley Davidson, 91
Hausser, 21, 109, 148
He-Man, 38
Heavy Car Mechanical Toys, 82
helicopters, *56*, 101–2
Herald Miniatures, 19, 20, 109–10, 136
Hill, John, & Co, 18, 50, 108–9, 148
Hillman Minx, *54*
Honda Motorcycle and Trailer, 91
Hornby,
    boats, 29
    trains, 118–25
Hornby Dublo, 123–4
Hornby, Frank, 52, 118–19
Hornby Hobbies, 124–5, 172–5
Horton, W., 18
Hot Wheels, 160
human figures, 17–19, 50, 106–11, 128, *135*, 143
    battery-operated, 25–6
    and see character toys; Britains
Humbrol Ltd, 128

Ichiko Co, 149
International Model Aircraft Ltd, 15, 87, 156

Jabberwock, *95*, 97
Jack in the Box, 73
Jaguar cars, *34*, 59, 75, 87, 143, 163
Japanese toy development, 25, 96
jeeps, *84*
Johillco *see* John Hill Co
John Bull printing outfits, 141
John Hill Co, 18, 50, 108–9, 148
Jouets de Strasbourg, 149
Joustra *see* Jouets de Strasbourg
Jumeau, 69–70

Kammer & Reinhardt, 67
KCO *see* Kellermann & Co
Kellermann & Co, 150
Kenner, 39
Kenner-Parker, 157, 167
Kidde Inc *see* Ertl
Kohnstam, 150–1
Konstructa kits, 41
Krackjack, 175

Lagonda, 77
lead toys, 143
    animal figures, 16–19
    characters, 37–8
    Disneyania, 64
    soldiers, 106–8, 143
    and see Britains; Timpo
Lego, 152
Lehmann, 89, 93–4, 152–3
Lesney Products, 53, 74–5, 130, 151, 153–4, 159

aeroplanes, 14
cars, *34*
character toys, *36*, 37
coronation coaches, 50–1, 130
Disneyania, *63*
motorcycles, 91
and see Matchbox
Leyland Octopus lorries, 59
Lilliput, 18, 136
Linemar, 154
Lines Brothers, 15, 97, 98, 155–7, 172
Liptons Tea Van, 78–9, *159*
Lone Ranger, 35
Lone Star *see* Die Casting Machine Tools Ltd (DCMT)
Lord Nelson engine, *119*, 121
lorries, *58*, 59, 78
Lotus Elan, 46
Lowko *see* Bassett-Lowke Ltd
Lyons Swiss Roll lorry, *58*

MAC700 Cyclist, *90*
Mac the motorcyclist, 95, 129
Macleans Toothpaste van, 87–8
magazines, 183
Magic Roundabout, *140*
Man from U.N.C.L.E., 47, *141*
Mangold, 32
Marklin, 125–6
Marks & Spencer toys, 82, 157
Marlines *see* Marx
Martin, 158
Marx, *35*, 64, 158–9
Masters of the Universe, 38
Matchbox Toys, 74–80, 151, 154, 159–60
    aeroplanes, 14
    cars, 35, 79
    character toys, 37, 39–40
    commercial vans, 78–9
    Dinky collection, 61, 79–80
    Disneyania, 64
    Miniatures, 80
    Models of Yesteryear, *76*, 77–9
    motorcycles, 91
    plastic kits, 101
    Superfast, 80
Matchless Toys Ltd, 91
Mattel Inc, 38–9, 49, 141, 160
Max Hand Werk, *71*
Meccano Ltd *and see* Dinky, 12, 52, 157, 160–1
    aeroplanes, 13–14, 15–16
    constructor kits, *11*, 40
    Hornby trains, 118–25
Meccano-Triang Ltd, 128
mechanical toys,
    banks, 23–4
    boats, 27–30
    cars, 31, 42–3, 82
    and see clockwork toys; novelty toys;
        Jouets de Strasbourg; Kellermann
Mercedes Benz, *33*, 77, 149
Merry-Go-Round, *132*
Merrythought Ltd, 162
Messerschmitt, 13
metal fatigue, 53–4
Mettoy Company *and see* Corgi, 41, 48, 81–2, 162–3
    aeroplanes, 14
    cars, 31
    motorcycles, 89
MGA, *31*
MGB, 59
Mickey Mouse, 38, 62, 63, 64, 65
Mighty Midgets, *130*, 131
military figures, 106–11 *and see* soldiers

military vehicles, 44, 61, *94*, *129*, *135 and see* Britains; Hausser
milk floats, 74, *133*
Minic, 83–9, 92, *95*, 97, 103, 156
Minnie Mouse, 38, 63, 65
missiles, 44
Model Home Farm Series, 16–17
Models Mini Ltd, 156, 163–4, 172
Models of Yesteryear, *75*, *76*, 77–9, 91, 154
Modern Toys (MT), 164
MOKO *see* Kohnstam
money boxes *see* banks
Monkeemobile 35–6, 47
Morestone *see* Morris & Stone
Morris cars, 42, 75, 103
Morris vans, 61
Morris & Stone (London) Ltd, 51, 91–2, 165–6
motorcycles, 95
  clockwork, 89–90, 95
  diecast, 90–2
  metal, 90
  plastic, 92
  tinplate, 89–90
  and see Alps; Arnold; Einfelt; Lesney; Tipp
Muffin the Mule, *36*, 37, 74
Muppets, 170
museums, 187

Noah's Arks, 21–2
Noddy, 145
Nomura Toys *see* T.N.
novelty toys,
  plastic, 96–7
  tinplate, 93–5, *153*
  and see Arnold; Asahi; Asekusa; Blomer & Schuler; Einfalt; Gunthermann; Lehmann; Linemar; Minic; Schreyer; T.N.; Tri-ang
NSU RO80, 59

Odell, Jack, 144, 153–4
Old Crocks *see* Charbens
Oldsmobile (Man from U.N.C.L.E.), 47, *141*
OMHL *see* Hausser
Osram lorry, 78

Palitoy, 167
paper toys, animal figures, 20
Paya, 31, *32*, 167–8
pedal cars, 98–9, 155, *157 and see* Lines Brothers
Pedigree Soft Toys Ltd, 168–9 *and see* Lines Brothers
Pelham Puppets, 170
Penguin, 87
penny toys, 100–1 *and see* Kellermann
petrol tankers, *159*
Phantom, 13, *34*
Pierottis, 67
Pinocchio, 64, 170
plastic kits, 101–2 *and see* constructor kits; Airfix; AMT; Bandai; Ertl
plastic toys, 102–3
  aeroplane construction kits, 15–16
  animal figures, 19–20
  boats, *29*, 29–30
  cars, 87–8, 171
  characters, 38–40
  construction kits, 101–2, 128, 130
  Disneyania, 63
  dolls, *169*
  motorcycles, 92
  novelty toys, 96–7

robots, *104*, 104–5
soldiers, 109–11, 128
trains, 124, 153
  and see Airfix; Britains; Ertl; Cowan de Groot; Lego; Minic; Models Mini; Pedigree Soft Toys; Ranlite; Scalextric; Toy Time Toys; Tri-ang
Playcraft Toys, 41 *and see* Corgi; Mettoy
Pocketoys, 134
Polar Sledge Team, 20
Polar Survey Party, 20
police cars, 143, *150*
Popeye, 35, 64
Postman Pat, 145
prices, 7–8 *and see* individual item
Prime Mover, 74
Princess Elizabeth train, 121–2
puppets, *36*, 170
Push and Go vehicles, 86
PW *see* Ichiko Co

racing cars, 143 *and see* cars
Radiant 5600, 175
radio-controlled boats, *29*
rag and bone cart, 74
railway accessories, 17–18, 34, 124, *158 and see* Britains; Meccano
railways *see* trains
Ranlite, 171
Raphael Tuck, 20
Rapido *see* Arnold Company
removal vans, 86, *87*
Revell, 101
Rice Krispies Van, *159*
Riley cars, 42, *54*, 57, *84*, 87
road roller, 74, 75, 153
Robbie the Robot, 104
robots, *25*, 104–5, *128 and see* Alps; Bandai; Cragstan; Daiya; Linemar; T.N.
rockets, 44 *and see* space toys
Roddy *see* Toy Time Toys
Rodnoid *see* Toy Time Toys
Rolls Royce cars, *54*, 59
Rosebud Ltd, 160
Rover, 42, 90
Rovex, 157
Royal Mail van, *55*
Royal Scot engine, *119*, 121

Saint, The, Volvo 1800, 45–6
Santa Claus, *132*
Santa Claus trade mark, 129
Scalex, 156, 163
Scalextric, 157, 172–3
Schreyer & Co, 32, *33*, 94, *95*, 173–4
Schuco *see* Schreyer & Co
Searchlight lorry, *134*
service stations, 86
SFBJ Societe de Fabrication des Bebes, 69
SG *see* Gunthermann
ships,
  diecast, 56–7, 88–9
  tinplate, *146*
  and see boats
shops, 183–4
Shuttle Craft, *112 and see* space toys
Simon & Halbig, *69*
Sindy doll, 168
Sir Nigel Greasley train, *121*, 123
Sky-Buster aeroplanes, 14
slot cars, 180
Snow White and the Seven Dwarfs, 37–8, 62, 64, *65*
soft toys *see* teddy bears; Steiff; Timpo
soldiers,
  diecast, 50, 108

index

Elastolin, *108*, 109
lead, 106–8, 143
plastic, 109–11, 128
and see Britains; Crescent; Hausser; Timpo
Sooty, 29
space toys, 38–9, 111–13, *142 and see* Alps; Bandai; Budgie; Dinky; T.N.
sparking flint mechanism, 128
Spitfire, 13
Spot-On, *34*, 35, 114–15, 157
Star Wars, 38–9
Startex, 156, 163
Steerable Driving School Car, 173–4
Steiff, 117–18, 175
Sting Ray, *102*
Structo *see* Ertl
Studebaker Golden Hawk, 44
Stuka, 13
submarines, *64*, 65
Sunbeam Alpine, 163
Sunbeam motorcycle, 91
Sunlight Soap van, *76*
Supercar, *166*
Superfast models, 80
Sutcliffe Pressings Ltd, 27–9, 176
Swoppets *see* W Britains Ltd

T Co *see* Tipp & Company
Talbot van, 78
Tammany Bank, *23*, 24
tank transporter set, 61
tanks *see* military vehicles
Taylor & Barratt, 51, 109
Technofix, 94 *and see* Einfalt
teddy bears, 116–18, *162 and see* Chad Valley; Merrythought; Steiff
Tekno, 92
television-related toys *see* character toys
Test Steer, 174
Texaco Tanker, *159*
Thomas the Tank Engine, 145
Thunderbirds, 39, *112*, 113
Timpo Toys, 109, 177
tinplate toys, 81–3, 83–9
aeroplanes, 10–12
animal figures, 20–1, *132*
boats, 27–30, *137*
cars, *26*, 31–3, 35–6, *83*, 84, *144*, 149, 163, 173–4
characters, 35–6
coronation coaches, 51
Disneyania, 64
motorcycles, 89–90
novelty toys, 93–5, *153*
penny toys, 100–1
robots, *104*
ships, 146
trains, 83–4, 118–26, *162*
and see Alps; Asahi; Asekusa; Bing; Blomer & Schuler; Brimtoy (Wells); Bub; Carette; Chad Valley; Distler; Einfalt; Fleishmann; Gunthermann; Hausser; Ichiko; Jouets de Strasbourg; Lehmann; Lines Brothers; Martin; Mettoy; Models Mini; Paya;

Scalextric; Schreyer; Sutcliffe Pressings; T.N.; Tipp
Tipp & Company, 81, *91*, 162, 177–8
Tippco *see* Tipp & Company
TM *see* Modern Toys (MT)
TMX Toys, 175
T.N., 178
Tonka, 39
Tootsietoy, 33, 179
toy fairs and swapmeets, 7, 182
Toy Time Toys Ltd, 179
Toyota (You Only Live Twice), 47
traction engines, 77–8
trains, 118–26
cast iron, 126
clockwork, 119–20
diecast, 118–26
electric, 120
plastic, 124, 153
tinplate, 83–4, 118–26, *162*
and see Bassett-Lowke; Bing; Brimtoy (Wells); Bub; Carette; Dinky; Hornby; Lehmann; Lines Brothers; Meccano; Mettoy; Tri-ang; Trix
Tri-ang, 29–30, 83, 124, 155, 161, 163 *and see* Minic
Triumph cars, 103, 180
Triumph motorcycles, 91
Trix, 126, 144, 178–9
Trojan vans, 61
trolley bus, *134*
TV Series range, *130*, 131
20,000 Leagues Under the Sea, *64*, 65

Ubilda, 138
Universal Matchbox, 154

valuations, 8 *and see* prices
Vanwall racing car, 143
VEBE/V.B./VEB/VB et cie *see* Bonnet et Cie
Venture boat, *28*, 29
Vickers Vanguard, *13*
Victory Industries, *30*, 180
village idiot, 19, *135*
Volvo 1800 (The Saint), 45–6
Vosper RAF Crash Tender, 180
Vulcan bomber, 13

Wallworks Company, 126
watches, 113
Wellings, Norah, 138
Wells Ltd, 31, 133
Westland helicopter, 101–2
Whizz Wheels, 48
wooden toys,
animal figures, 20, 21–2
arks, 21–1
boats, 27–8
and see Lines Brothers; Sutcliffe Pressings

Yeh, David, 159
Yellow Submarine, 47, *48*

Zebra Toys, 131
zoo animals *see* animal figures